"...a portrait _ an
legend. As I read the story I felt as though I had the
privilege of meeting Johnny Luster. For those who
love Alaska, the outdoors and adventure, Luster is
the kind of man you hope in some way you could
emulate." –*Aaron Whitt*

A read not to be passed over. Johnny Luster is truly a
Mountain Man. His closeness and understanding of
nature is to be envied, and his experiences will hold
your attention to the very last page. –*Avril Johannes*

"...the life of a man with the heartfelt drive and skills
to stand alone on a plot of mountain scree where no
other human dared to venture, undoubtedly trying to
embrace the very quality in mankind that has been
slowly supressed by civilization–the "mountain man"
grit. –*Larry Bartlett,* author of *Float Hunting Alaska*

Despite the hardships he endured, Johnny managed
to find his place in the world and build a life that
allowed him to live his dreams...
...his love of the land reaches out from the pages of
the story and makes one realize how "being rich" can
mean many different things. What a wonderful life
story of an extraordinary pioneer. –*Anya Petersen/Frey*

Out of Season bridges America's all-but-forgotten frontier past, as the memories and adventurous tales of those born early in the last century are fading away. Mary Adams has captured a glimpse of the kind of history that, if not captured in books, is lost to us forever. *Out of Season* is a vintage Alaskan adventure story and an insightful synthesis of Native American history to boot. —*Charles D. Hayes*, author of *Portals in a Northern Sky*

Johnny Luster

-oil painting by Beth Libbey

OUT OF SEASON
The Johnny Luster Story

**Tribute by Charles Elliott,
Senior Editor for *Outdoor Life***

Mary E. Adams

Northern Publishing, Wasilla, Alaska

Out of Season:
The Johnny Luster Story
by Mary E. Adams

Northern Publishing
P.O. Box 871803
Wasilla, AK 99687
TonyRuss.com for orders

10 9 8 7 6 5 4 3

ISBN 0-9639869-7-x
LCCN 2003104052
Edited by Tony Russ and Diane O'Loughlin
Cover Design by Paul Moon, Moon & Stars Communications, moonstars@alaska.com, 907-223-2938
Oil painting by Beth Libbey, 907-357-6040, info@saddletrailsnorth.com

To my husband Bob, who loved Alaska more than
any man I ever knew.

Acknowledgements

Many thanks to various friends and acquaintances of Johnny Luster who were instrumental in seeing this project through.
–Mary Elizabeth Adams
Wasilla, Alaska

Contents

A TRIBUTE TO JOHNNY LUSTER

by his long-time friend and hunting partner
Charles Elliott
–Senior Editor, *Outdoor Life*

John Luster was the focal point of a dramatic and unforgettable adventure in my life. This was so long ago that now it seems to have occurred in another life.

We were youngsters then–by today's measurements at least. Both of us, in our early forties, were camped in the high, rugged Talkeetna Mountains, more isolated and wild than they are now. From where we were camped in the lofty ranges, we could see big game animals any hour of the day. Almost always in sight were white Dall sheep filing along a precipice, or a mountain goat or two looking down from a towering pinnacle, or herds of caribou drifting past or big grizzlies feeding on the wealth of early fall blueberries–a hunter's paradise!

As I remember, Johnny was relatively new to Alaska. He had brought up a string of saddle and pack horses from Wyoming, his home state, and was camp wrangler for Jim Simpson, our outfitter for this Alaska safari. Four hunters were in our party and Simpson had managed to round up a guide for each of us–men who were hunters on their own, but who had little or no experience in the guiding business. John Luster had more mountain savvy and woodsmanship than all of the others pooled together. But his job with the horses was more important because this was the first—or almost the first—packsaddle big game hunt in Alaska's history.

As our horse wrangler, Johnny didn't do any guiding, but I was quick to see how excellent a mountain man and woodsman he was, so when we were in camp, I spent as much time as possible with him. He was a quiet fellow, not much of a talker, and I didn't know his real background until years later.

I got an impressive indication of it, however, after we had been in camp for a number of days.

Early in the hunt we had taken some good trophies—or at least what inexperienced tyros from Georgia considered "good"—but the weather was unusually warm for that time of year in the Alaska mountains.

We had many more days ahead of us on the hunt, did not want any spoiled meat on our hands, so the guides suggested that they take off a couple of days, pack the meat out to Chickaloon on the main road and truck it to cold storage in Palmer.

To this we agreed. It gave us at least a day or two to relax around camp.

Charles Elliott (on right) preparing for one of the first horseback big game hunts in Alaska's history.

I could not see two entire days of being parked on my can in a tent or on a log, so next morning after the guides pulled out with our meat, I climbed to the top of the rock cliff blocking one side of our campsite. I found a comfortable rock and parked my carcass there to glass the countryside for any unusual happenings.

The customary sight of sheep crossing a cliff or a rock slide, and caribou grazing on an open slope were a part of the landscape, but I saw no record trophies among them. Then my glasses picked up a large grizzly feeding in a patch of blueberries a couple of miles away on a mountain slope across the creek.

From the top of the bluff I yelled for John to saddle the horses. I scrambled back to camp, threw two or three loose shells in my pocket and John, I and another hunter rode to the foot of the ridge on which I had seen the grizzly.

The other hunter walked up a hollow paralleling the ridge in case we spooked the bear in that direction. Then, John and I climbed to where I had seen the foraging grizzly. It was still there facing at an angle toward us and I shot for the heart.

The bear went down, then bounced to its feet and ran over the side of the ridge. We sprinted to a nearby high point and a couple of hundred yards below us saw the grizzly stand up and look back.

I shot again for the heart and the bear went down, then stood up. It went down on my third shot and again stood up. At my next shot, it lurched a step forward and wrapped its arms around a small tree.

"He's dead on his feet" John said, "but that's not the bear we shot at first."

We picked up the blood trail of the first bear and found it lying under a bunch of brush, watching us. It wasn't dead. I shot again and knocked the grizzly on its side. Its feet were waving in the air and it looked very much alive.

I checked my rifle. I didn't remember loading, but had no more shells in my pocket and only one in my gun. We were standing less than 30 feet from the wounded animal.

Johnny did not have a gun.

"If I could see his head well enough," I said, "I'd finish him off."

"John picked up a rock and threw it to where the bear lay. Instead of raising his head, as we expected, the big grizzly suddenly rolled to all fours and charged us, bawling with a roar that shook the earth.

I knew I had to get the crosshairs on its head. If I didn't shatter his skull, this was it.

The grizzly was within 25 feet. John thought I'd frozen at the controls and he acted quickly. He yelled and waived his arms. The shout and motion diverted the bear's attention and it turned away from me and toward my partners, who took off up the mountain like timber wolves.

In its weakened condition the bear didn't run more than a few yards, then turned and went back to its spot under the brush. I could see its head plainly now. Taking my time, I put the crosshairs between its eyes and carefully squeezed off a shot.

The grizzly flattened out and lay still. "Let's let him die good and dead" I suggested, "while we go see what happened to the other grizzly."

Our other hunter had come up and was standing over the second bear, a very large silvertip that had made its last gasp. We skinned it out and packed it on my shoulders with a sort of diamond hitch to get it to the horses. I handed my rifle to the hunter.

"Better let Johnny carry it" he said.

He loaded a couple of shells into the rifle, handed it to Luster and made his way with me and my heavy load, down the drain to where we had tied our horses.

In the meantime, Luster climbed the mountain to where we had left our first supposedly dead grizzly. Within 20 feet of it, the big bear suddenly reared up, towering over the guide. John threw up the rifle and shot it point blank in the chest.

The 220 grain bullet seemed to have no effect whatsoever. The grizzly roared and lunged at Luster, but swatted only empty air where the guide had been a fraction of a second before.

Running down the mountain, the bear only shirt-tail distance behind and roaring with every swipe of his heavy claws, John frantically jacked the last shell into the chamber of the rifle. Holding it back over his shoulder, with the end of the barrel almost touching the grizzly's head, he jerked the trigger and ran for his life.

Fortunately, that last chunk of lead broke the grizzly's neck. When we arrived with the horses thirty minutes later, Luster was still sitting on the mountainside, thirty yards above the grizzly, throwing rocks at the dead bear, to be sure there was no sign of life left in it.

Before Johnny Luster's time, packsaddle hunts were unknown in Alaska. His pioneering spirit helped forge the way for others to follow.

John Luster chose to stay and live in Alaska. Shortly after he drove down his permanent stakes, he became a registered guide and in the next few decades became Alaska's most popular big game outfitter.

For years he spent his winters running a trapline far beyond the end of the trail, often in weather that howled around him at 60 below zero.

At this writing he is in his late eighties and apparently as tough as he was when the grizzly tried to get close enough to pat him on his behind. His eyesight remains as sharp as that of an eagle, no whisper of sound escapes his hearing and he can climb a vertical trail all day.

Not long ago a doctor friend persuaded John to take a physical examination.

"They put me on one of them machines" Johnny said, "where you walk and run and don't go anywhere. So I walked and then ran and after I'd been doing that awhile, Doc stopped the machine and said 'Get down. If a horse don't fall on you or you don't get buried in an avalanche, you'll live for another hundred years. Then they'll have to hit you with a pole ax when they get ready to bury you.'"

If not the last, John Luster is one of the last of the real, old-time mountain men. Even in his lifetime he has become a legend in his adopted—but now his native—state.

Mary Adams has written a glowing account of his life. It makes a fellow such as I wish I had been privileged to spend many more days with this old mountain man on the trail.

–CHARLES ELLIOTT

Johnny Luster in his element–riding his horse through his mountains.

FOREWORD

When I first met Johnny Luster he was in prison. At least, he considered it a prison. At 85, he was living in a small cabin some three miles out of Wasilla, Alaska perched on a hill surrounded by snow-capped mountains. It was a comfortable place, with a modern kitchen and a wood stove, and secluded enough that you couldn't see another house anyway you looked. But for a man who had lived his life making camp in the wilderness, this was too civilized.

"My kids was after me to see the homestead I had up on the Chickaloon river. They said 'Sell it, sell it.' So I says, 'Okay, sell it!' And so I was gone somewhere, and when I come back they had sold it and tied up to this place here. Shoot, a fellow would die right here—nothing to do and no place to go, because if I hook up my dogs I'll get out on the road and get run over."

I looked below his cabin at the dog team scattered underneath big birch trees, each one with his own separate dog house. A sled was sitting nearby.

"It's all right to come down once in awhile to take a swim." he fussed, shaking his head. But then he let slip his apparent intention to leave—permanently: "I got a place back there on Caribou Creek—a deeded piece of land from the Federal Government. It's now in a caribou reserve and they says I'll never have no neighbors—which is good."

It was obvious I had discovered a true mountainman.

Partly out of curiosity and partly thinking this would be a good way of passing off another cold Alaskan winter day, I had gathered up my tape recorder, camera and notebooks and stopped by to pick up Rose and Milton Menard—who had set up my interview with this illustrious legend. It was cold, and the snow was deep.

We headed east down the Parks Highway through Wasilla, a small town about forty miles from Anchorage if you follow the Glenn highway skirting the (Cook) inlet—ten miles as the crow flies. White mountains towered high above the valley floor on three sides, with the Knik River snaking its way southwestward to the inlet waters of the Cook.

The incredible beauty of the Matanuska-Susitna Valley was a breath-stealing experience, almost too beautiful. One sometimes felt as if it were unreal, something you dreamed of in your sleep, or saw hanging in some art gallery. Yet, in spite of being there and living amongst its splendor, there were moments of guilt when I would take my surroundings for granted, like they weren't even there. The mountains themselves seemed to know and sense my lack of admiration, painting their peaks a livid pink with the rays of the setting sun, just to let me know they were around.

We turned left off the Parks onto a side road skirting a small hill and drove about two miles before we came to a driveway going up a butte at about a 45-degree angle.

"That's it!" cried Milton.

It looked like solid ice. I held my breath and shifted gears–there was no slowing down now. We slid sideways a brief second, then roared up the slope. The road ended abruptly in Johnny Luster's back yard. I sat there a second, catching my breath–we had made it! (A rather common realization for Alaskans.)

Johnny turned out to be a complete surprise. I had expected to see an old sourdough, tough and grizzled, with white beard and huge frame. From all the hype I had heard, I had envisioned another Paul Bunyan–yet here he was, a small man with sand-colored hair and beard, who walked with a slight limp and stooped shoulders.

It was his eyes that caught you–deep blue, with hints of mischievousness, yet they almost spoke to you as they gave off hints of childlike honesty.

He invited us inside the warm cabin. I no sooner walked through the door when I looked up to see a certificate on the wall that caught my attention:

———————————

THE ALASKA LEGISLATURE
honoring
Johnny Luster

The members of the Fifteenth Alaska State Legislature honor Johnny Luster, world renown Chickaloon Mountain Man, guide and outfitter.

Johnny was born in 1905 on the Wind River Indian reservation in Wyoming. Born a halfbreed Shoshone, he grew up with the wild horses.

In the 1930's, Johnny had a short film career as an Indian warrior in several of John Wayne's westerns. In the early 1940's, Johnny caught 20 horses and headed for Alaska, the Great Land.

Johnny settled in the Chickaloon River Valley in the mountains north of Palmer where he found rich soil and abundant game. He raised 12 children and lived off the land, his sole income from hunting and trapping.

Johnny has spent almost his entire life in the wild. At 82 he works a trapline by dog sled each winter. He is still an active big game guide and continues to lead adventurous horseback tours into the wilderness.

We are fortunate to have an Alaskan like Johnny in our midst and we applaud his pioneering spirit.

———

It was signed by the Speaker of the House and the President of the Senate, and dated May 15, 1987.

Impressive. But not quite accurate.

"They made a mistake on it. It was 1904. I thought it was 1905, but I went down to see my brother on the reservation—me and him are the only two that survived out of the family—and he said 'No, it was March 22, 1904,' " he remarked.

While Johnny brewed up a pot of coffee, I wandered about the room. In one corner lay a pair of snowshoes, some traps, and a dog sled harness–tools of the trade. On the wall were dozens of pictures taken on various hunting expeditions–hunters with their trophies of Dall sheep, caribou, moose, and grizzly bears.

"I used to have some muscles on me. Now I'm getting shrank up," he muttered. "Just gotta get some exercise, that's what I need. I'll be young again pretty soon–about a couple of weeks. Quick drinking coffee–that knocks the daylights out of you."

I noticed he always smiled after a good quip–a man with a sense of humor, not unlike that of the famed Will Rogers.

And so began a series of interviews over the next few months. I would discover an incredible story, little realizing just what a rare gem was before me–a man whose lifetime has spanned half the history of the American West, whose roots were immersed in the flavor and color of times long since vanished, yet who somehow survived the cultural changes of modern civilization with his lifestyle intact.

This is his story, as best I can tell it. There were parts of his life he would not comment on until pressed–his voice falling off to a mere whisper: "and that was that..."

Much of what is written has been researched from rare books, accounts of reservation life and the events that molded Johnny into his unique personality. I have tried to capture his ways; characterizing his true self by using verbatim quotations from the tapes, for they show us a colorful and delightful man–unlike any in the world today.

–MARY ELIZABETH ADAMS

Johnny loved to ride his horses, and take his dog with him.

1
"GRANDFATHER"

"Loyalty was not always fair in its demands..."

It is not often that men will, in their lifetimes, find what it is they are looking for. Usually they pass by it, never realizing it was before them all the while. They would spend their days chasing the fabled "end of the rainbow," sometimes destroying forever the lives of other contented and wise souls caught in their pathway.

Such was the case for the American Indian.

For centuries the tribes had lived in the great wilderness unmolested and unaffected by the rest of the world. They had no knowledge of the Industrial Age which was upon them, nor did they know that there were large cities with rich merchants They did not know their world contained vast oceans that were now carrying the sailing vessels of explorers and pale-skinned immigrants heading their direction. How could they have known that these same people would view them as ignorant savages, to be "enlightened and refined" and forced to stand aside as docile children while they came ashore to claim their lands as their own?

Self-evident truths were not all that "self-evident" in regards to the red man, for in spite of all the idealistic and noble declarations these men would eventually sign in the halls of Philadelphia and Washington, they meant little in view of the vast treasures of gold, furs, and land there for the taking. Cries of "freedom" and "liberty" somehow stopped at Indian boundary lines.

No doubt there were warnings. In the council huts, great chiefs discussed their visions from "Wakan"–as the Sioux referred to "the spirit from the other world." But even visions could not prepare them for men of such ruthless treachery and cunning appetite. Would "locusts" speak of drought, or a devouring horde of white-faced animals? And what were those iron sticks that spoke with puffs of smoke and made loud noises?

It would be some time before he could interpret these visions correctly, and for now he could only ponder their meanings. But even if he could have discerned his visions and dreams, he was powerless to stop what was coming. His way of life will have vanished when his great-grandchildren became old enough to understand the traditions and ceremonies of their culture.

And so they came. First the fur traders and trappers. Then the explorers, which returned east with talk that would further stir the fantasies and whet the appetites of a restless young nation. They came by the thousands, cautiously snaking their way across Indian lands, wide-eyed but resolute–driven by fantasy, greed, and a sense of adventure. The deluge was unstoppable. Trails were littered and scarred with abandoned possessions, rotting animal carcasses, and pitiful gravesites. They brought with them their deadly diseases and plagues which would kill Indians by the thousands.

The "locusts" had arrived.

There was, however, one place that (temporarily at least) halted this madness. It was a large mass of mountain range, which extended itself from Alaska through Mexico, vertically cutting a path down the North American continent like the wall of China. "The Continental Divide" (as it was called) would serve the same purpose as Jim Bowie's famous line etched in the Alamo sand, a decision point at which men were forced to consider their last chance to return back across the flat plains to civilization and all its benefits...to family and roots...to latest fashions and finishing schools–all the comforts of city life. At this halfway point to the California gold fields or Oregon home-steads, wagon trains were halted temporarily to obtain fresh provisions and mend their wagons before attempt-ing the hazardous mountain passes. These majestic peaks stood towering into the blue sky, silently whis-pering words to a man's spirit that questioned and chal-lenged his commitment to his dreams. It would be here, as he stood with his face into the setting sun and pon-dered the unknown that lay ahead, that he would learn who and what he was, and choose his destiny accord-ingly.

A few men—not many—had stood in this same place and discovered that they were not inclined to go forward or backward. What more could a man want than to enjoy the incredible beauty and provision of these mountains themselves?

Strong, and confident in himself, he was willing to learn from these so-called "savages," impressed by their vast knowledge of nature and their uncanny ability to survive in it. This vision of a life not complicated by the restrictive ideas of civilization, but of freedom and independence to pursue manhood in its highest form, was to become the thing that gave birth to all the legendary "Mountainmen"–men who chose neither the gold of Sacramento, nor the fertile soil of Oregon, but accepted the "decision line" itself as their life's dream.

Such were the likes of men such as Jim Bridger, Jedediah Smith, Kit Carson and hundreds of others. Many would become legends in their lifetimes, even though few would understand their strange behavior or choice of lifestyle. Most would marry Indian wives, father their children in tribal tepees or in mountain caves, and roam the vast wilderness as if it were an Eden created only for themselves.

Johnny's grandfather, William Merritt Leister (the name was later changed to Luster) carried within him the genes of the "Mountainman." He had arrived in the late 1840's, having left his roots in the soil of Kentucky. His father had migrated west into Daniel Boone's "great meadow" from the Colonies during the Revolutionary War, when thousands of would-be settlers wore a beaten path along the Cumberland Gap to the Ohio River.

But the thread stretched further back than that–to men who had left England for a new life with promise of opportunity. It was as if their very bones were made of iron and a huge magnet lay hidden in the mountains of the West, drawing them with an irresistible force. Now, several generations later, this same force brought William to his "mother lode," and the name "Luster" to another home.

We know little about William Luster's life in the Indian lands, except that he roamed southwestward from Kentucky into Arkansas, Colorado, and Utah. Eventually he made his way into the Wind River country of Wyoming, where the "Valley of the warm winds" ran through western central Wyoming near the main range of the Rockies. Men who kept diaries during this time spoke of constant movement–making camp in shelters, tending to pack horses, hunting game for food and trapping animals for pelts.

Like others, he took an Indian wife–a Shoshone. But unlike many "squaw men" who lived with their women without benefit of clergy, they were married in a civil ceremony. Later, reservation requirements would make this mandatory, but William had enough moral fiber to feel it was both honorable and right, no matter if he was far from home and social responsibilities.

"He thought an awful lot of her," Johnny said.

Shoshone women were generally treated cruelly, their men often beating them so severely that they were killed or their faces gashed and noses cut off. Shoshone men did not have a keen eye for beauty nor feel their women deserved any sympathy, so in this atmosphere she was indeed fortunate to have William Luster for a husband.

Together they had two children, John and Francina. For a brief time afterward William would escape the tangled web of civilization and develop within himself a mature confidence typical of the scraggly trail guide. He had a hardness like a piece of leather, not gruff or rude, but possessing a certain look that told a man "Here was someone who would never back down from anything–no matter how big." And he would pass this characteristic on to his son.

Proud of his family, William would often share his innermost feelings in letters home, though he knew what "society" thought of his marriage. He would talk, almost reverently, about the mountains. This was the place his heart and soul lived–the place of elk and beaver, sheep and antelope, the place of lofty peaks and snow-capped mountains, immense river valleys and sparkling lakes. It was that thing which would keep a man young inside all his days, long after his strength had gone and fire no longer kept him warm.

And so this adventuresome and satisfying life surrounded William Luster's small and loving family. They learned a lot from the Shoshones: how the cries of the coyote when the moon was full meant good luck; and how they must watch for NINIMBEBS, the little devils with red noses, who dressed in mountain sheepskins decorated with bright colors and who carried quivers of invisible arrows. They would also learn never to kill the chickadee, for it was he who had discovered the world and to kill one was bad luck, and that the creator of the world was DAM-AP-WA, or Father-God, who had pulled out the upper teeth of the elk because elk were meant to be eaten by Indians, not Indians by elk.

The Shoshones were not a plains people. Their roots lay in the bleak Great Basin country of Nevada and eastern California. Later migrations north had led them across the Rockies and into the Dakotas where they carried on a continual feud with the Blackfeet, Crows and Hidatsas. In the 1700's however, the Shoshones acquired horses through the Utes and Comanches, which gave them the ability to overpower their enemies and also to hunt buffalo more effectively. This edge lasted for some time until other tribes acquired guns and the Shoshones were driven back into the mountain valleys. This is where they were when Lewis and Clark sought them in hopes of acquiring pack animals for their journey into Oregon. (It had been a Shoshone maiden, Sacagawea, who had led them to her brother, the tribal chief.) So when other pale-faced men arrived, the Shoshones were already familiar with "tab-ba-bone," the word Sacagawea had given for "stranger" or "white man," and were generally docile and accommodating to them.

But the raw, untamed paradise of Shoshone country kept men isolated from major events and focused, rather, on life among the Indians and the skirmishes between the tribes. William knew only vaguely of the events taking place in the rest of the country, nor could he have known the significant times in which he lived. Many interlocking events were weaving themselves together to form the embryo of a great and powerful nation. Texas had been annexed following a war with Mexico. Mark Twain was writing his famous *Life on the Mississippi*. The Mormons had established their colony in Utah. But the Indians were not yet immersed into the world of the "tab-ba-bone," and except for the five civilized tribes of the eastern states, were not involved with, nor even aware of, the gathering storm clouds along the Mason-Dixon line some thousand miles to the east.

When news of the Civil War came, the clash at Ft. Sumter rocked the West. The alarm spread quickly along the fabled Pony Express and relayed itself into the tepees and camps of the mountainmen. Letters from home came with urgent and frightened voices. Mark Twain wrote of his feelings from Virginia City:

> Out West there was a good deal of confusion in men's minds during the first months of the great trouble, a good deal of unsettledness, of leaning this way, then that, then the other way. It was hard for us to get our bearings.

Suddenly, plans for the Transcontinental Railroad were put on hold, and prospects for development were tabled. Men were painfully discovering that the roots of the past were suddenly invading their new territory, exposing ties that could not be easily severed.

It would be easy to stay in the mountains...and many did. But there was a sense of painful frustration tormenting William's mind. Loyalty was not always fair in its demands, and the price to be paid would be enormous–for it would shatter their whole world, especially his wife and children's, who had never seen Kentucky. They could not share his agony nor appreciate his concern. Yet to totally leave his relatives and loved ones to whatever fate lay ahead would betray a total lack of honor. He would have to return.

And so, William Merritt Luster did return to the banks of the Ohio and brought with him his wife and two children. It was not the kind of introduction he had wanted for them, for he had little time to renew acquaintances nor view the many changes that had taken place since he had left, for Union forces were already massing at Cairo, some thirty miles down river.

After making arrangements for them to stay with relatives, William said his goodbyes, taking aside his young son for a short walk along the edge of the woods. They talked about home–the West, the traplines they would set when they got back and the elk they would hunt. It would only be for a little while and the war would soon end.

Running his hand through his son John's coal-black hair as a gesture of comfort, he smiled and nudged his small chin with his big hands—everything would be back like it was—he'd see. Then mounting his horse, he waved goodbye and headed westward for Columbus to join with the Confederate forces there, less than fifty miles from Paducah.

On both sides, men were eager for battle. Grant's army had endured the restless and muddy hell-hole of Cairo across the river for some months, waiting for the first engagement with Paducah. It would be an easy victory. But ironically, North and South were to test each other over a worthless three-shack hamlet called Belmont, Kentucky. Had it been of strategic value, or even served as a psychological or moral-boosting ploy, some sense might have been made of the ridiculous slaughter of some 600 soldiers on both sides. A detachment of soldiers had been sent from Columbus to meet Grant's probe, which the Confederate generals felt was nothing but a decoy. William had been among them and became one of the first to die.

His body was still warm as the victory celebration began. With a great display of cannon volleys, shouting and revelry, the Union band—in the most incredulous act of all—quickly began a sickly concert–a practice detested by Grant.

When word of his death reached his wife two days later, the little Indian woman who had given him such happiness said nothing, but as was sometimes typical of the Shoshone way, took a knife and cut her hair, sliced off the end of her little finger, covered her head with her blanket and died that same day. The year was 1861.

2
THE WHITE MAN'S ROAD

"When I turn to the west, the approaching night hides all..."

During the remaining years of the Civil War, the West lay like a dormant bulb waiting for the end of a long, dark winter. It was not quiet, by any means, but the "Indian problem" had been shelved temporarily until the end of hostilities–troops were needed elsewhere.

Confederates had been denied benefits to the Homestead Act, but others continued the westward advance. Farmers settled in Kansas and Nebraska, and there were many deserters and defeated Southerners who looked to the Northwest for fresh opportunities. Across the midwestern states there was terror, as the band of renegade guerrillas, led by Quantrell, vented savage revenge, giving rise to the outlaw gangs of Jesse James and Cole Younger.

The Pony Express had been replaced by the more economical telegraph lines and Wells, Fargo and Company had built up a thriving transportation business which was served by William Cody, later to be known as "Buffalo Bill." In Virginia City, the Comstock Lode treasures had helped to finance the war.

But the Indians were not happy when rations promised by treaties were delayed "because of preoccupation with Civil War problems." There were several massacres in Minnesota and at Sand Creek, Colorado by the Sioux, which prompted calvary to send urgent calls for assistance. In general, the West was in a time of lawlessness and atrocity, with little relief in sight.

John and Francina had witnessed the War on all sides, even though Kentucky had begun the conflict as a neutral state. The half-breed orphans had lived with relatives following the traumatic deaths of their parents, but this did not shield them from the brutal horrors of battles as the maimed returned home with missing limbs and blinded eyes, and grief-ridden wives mourned their losses.

John had been ten years old when they had arrived in Paducah; his sister, eight. Now he was a lanky sixteen–dark-complected like his mother, and subject to certain taunts.

These had been years of pain he wanted to forget, and what was left of childhood memories lay somewhere in the West. Flashes of tranquil deer and elk grazing in alpine meadows had kept alive his dream to return. He had never spent a day without thinking about it.

The Indian tribes were also doing a lot of thinking...

The Shoshones were divided into four groups: the Bannocks, the Tukuarikas, the Lemhis and the Shoshones proper. Portions of both the Eastern and Western Shoshones resided in Idaho, but the allies were divided on what to do about the "White Man." The aggressive Bannocks considered the wagon trains fair game and took up the terrorist activity where the Sioux left off. By 1840, the buffalo had begun to recede from the Idaho Snake River country through Yellowstone Park into Montana–the domain of the dreaded Blackfeet. So for protection, the Bannocks and Shoshones hunted together–the majority wintering in the Bear River valley. After the hunting season of 1862, Chief Washakie of the Eastern Shoshones pulled out. He was not interested in carrying on the marauding any longer and left for the Salmon River area. But the Bannocks and other rebellious tribesmen persisted in their attacks until the Calvary, located at Fort Douglas near Salt Lake, swooped down in a decisive battle, killing almost four hundred Indians–including men, women and children. "We took no prisoners," they reported. It broke forever the force of the Bannock nation.

The intervening years of 1863-1869 became the Treaty Period between the United States and the various bands of Bannock and Shoshones. Chief Washakie's band had already adopted a policy of coexistence with the white man (one of the first to do so), and in 1866 there were almost 2,000 Eastern Shoshones in the Green River valley of Wyoming. Four years later all of the Indians except Washakie's band would be driven out of that state.

The West was to change rapidly after the war. Without asking, men were already assuming the Indian lands to be theirs–whether now or at some later date, it was just a matter of time. And so, for the most part, their impressions of it tended to revolve around its eventual use for railroads, towns and commercial ventures. A small army of surveyors were busy mapping the territories to that end.

John left Kentucky around 1867, leaving behind his younger sister, who would be adopted by another family and be raised in the Eastern states. Heading westward into Arkansas, where he hoped to lay claim to a piece of land his father had purchased years before, he met and married a young Scottish girl, Lucy Benson. Together they hoped to farm that land, but learned that it had been taken over by others, who had managed to "arrange" title into their favor. So John and Lucy left Arkansas by wagon and traveled northward into Colorado, where he farmed, and eventually got a job as a policeman in Trinidad. Eventually, John and Lucy made it back to the Wind River country by wagon, this time to a reservation system, where they built a sod-roofed house with a dirt floor, began farming a homestead, and started raising a family.

"Dad was an awful hard worker–he worked too hard. That was rare for anybody who was part-Indian"

Johnny recalled.

He also gained a reputation as a man who never backed down, even single-handedly breaking up a free-for-all coal miner's battle by facing down the shotgun-toting leader with nothing more than fearless determination.

"If you mean it, look 'em in the eye and talk with a l-o-w, s-l-o-w voice," he would tell his sons. This advice would never be forgotten by Johnny.

The Indian wars were not yet over, however, as the great flood of migrants had swelled the population of trans-Mississippi west from fewer than seven million to more than sixteen million. This overwhelming wave of human conquest would give rise to more than 928 recorded clashes between the Indians and the white man before the reservation system swallowed them whole. It was a tragic and sad time.

Old warriors made speeches:

> My sun is set. My day is done. Darkness is stealing over me. Before I lie down to rise no more, I will speak to my people. Hear me, for this is not the time for me to tell a lie. The Great Spirit made us, and gave us this land we live in. He gave us the buffalo, antelope and deer for food and clothing. Our hunting grounds stretched from the Mississippi to the great mountains. We were free as the winds and heard no man's commands. We fought our enemies, and feasted our friends. Our braves drove away all who would take our game. They captured women and

horses from our foes. Our children were many and our herds were large. Our old men talked with spirits and made good medicine. Our young men hunted and made love to the girls. Where the tepee was, there we stayed, and no house imprisoned us. No one said, "To this line is my land, to that is yours." We gave him meat and presents, and told him go in peace. He looked on our women and stayed to live in our tepees. His fellows came to build their roads across our hunting grounds. He brought with him the magic water that makes men foolish. With his trinkets and beads he even bought the girl I loved. I said, "The White Man is not a friend, let us kill him." But their numbers were greater than blades of grass. They took away the buffalo and shot down our best warriors. They took away our lands and surrounded us by fences. Their soldiers camped outside with cannon to shoot us down. They wiped the trails of our people from the face of the prairies. They forced our children to forsake the ways of their fathers. When I turn to the east I see no dawn. When I turn to the west, the approaching night hides all.

The Paiute Chief Wovoka, like Chief Washakee, could see the futility of further resistance:

Hoo-oo! My children, my children! In days behind I called you to travel the hunting trail or to follow the war trail. Now these trails are choked with sand, they are covered with grass. The

young men cannot find them. Today I call upon
you to travel a new trail, the only trail now open,
The White Man's Road...

The Sioux uprising over the Dakota Black Hills
in which Custer's calvary force of 246 were killed, led
to the eventual defeat of the Indian. There would be
relentless, ruthless vengeance until all Indians were
herded into reservation lands, where they suffered from
shrinking allotments of food, clothing and other sup-
plies promised them by a fickle and self-serving Con-
gress. They knew little or nothing about farming, and
most of the land they had been allotted was too arid for
subsistence, much less for profit.

But perhaps more pitiful was the deathblow to the
Indian spirit which came, not only from the White Man,
but from their own Shamans.

In 1889, a Paiute Shaman announced that he had a
visit from the Great Spirit in heaven that told him a
time was coming when the buffalo would fill the plains
and dead tribesmen would be restored to their families. They would then live a blissful life, free of the
White Man and his works. He assured his followers
that if they would adhere to certain precepts and per-
form the proper ritual dance (called the Ghost Dance
by whites), they would have a vision of this marvelous
world soon to come.

This Ghost Dance cult spread across the western
reservations like a whirlwind. By 1890, many of the
Sioux abandoned everything to dance day and night,

giving rise to the apprehensions of Agency officials. Eventually, though he was not convinced of the vision, Sitting Bull was singled out as behind the Sioux dancing. He was ordered arrested, and during a rescue attempt he was killed, along with six policemen. Some 400 of his warriors fled southward to the Cheyenne River reservation, 38 of them taking refuge with Chief Big Foot. Worried about the approaching troops, these Indians fled and made camp at a place called Wounded Knee. The next morning, 500 troopers surrounded their camp and commenced firing, slaughtering the fleeing Indians. They cut down men, women and children until the snow was colored a bright crimson. Afterwards, men who made up the burial party were paid $2 for each body thrown naked into a pit and buried.

The hope that had been raised by the Ghost Dance faltered and finally vanished, and with it the Indian's last dreams for a return to yesterday. Chief Washakie had been right. Perhaps he had seen the futility long ago, and through wiser eyes accepted the inevitable. Now they must learn the White Man's ways–not as better, but as their only hope for survival. The pain would be felt for many years to come, perhaps never lost entirely.

Several years later, a white man visiting a reservation happened to mention that he owned a buffalo skin, one that had come down from olden times. First, an old Indian man paid him a visit and asked to see and touch the skin. Soon, with a silent reverence and humility, others also came and knelt before the sacred object, to touch its deep fur and pray. Even the sick were brought into its presence. All that was left were memories...

3
"JOHNNY TWO-FEATHERS"

"Here am I, neither an Indian nor a white man...just nothing..."

We come now to the subject of our story.

Johnny Luster had been born in late March, 1904, one of the last of John and Lucy's twelve children, all born on the Wind River Reservation. It was the same time that the famous Tom Horn had been hung–for these were the days of range wars, vigilante armies, cattle rustling and lynchings. Violence was all around them in one form or another.

Powerful cattle barons had swallowed up the Indian lands and replaced the buffalo, which they had hunted to near-extinction, with thousands of cattle from Texas. Great cattle drives from the South had brought immense herds North to fatten on these ranges. But over-grazing had led to great losses, and ranchers were blaming sheepherders, rustlers, and small farmers for their problems. Eventually there was bloodshed. It was a day of savage vengeance. Johnny described how it was:

> In the early days, that story about when they stand up and face one another, that was all a lie. Most everybody that was killed, somebody waylayed 'em on the hill there, or they just walked out and shot 'em. I know, 'cause I was there. I never ambushed nobody. If you couldn't face 'em, that quick-draw stuff was for the birds. I know of different killins that happened. This fellow was really stuck on this girl, and she married a good guy, and then he got to drinking a bit and was gonna get behind his horse and shoot him when he came out of the house. The fellow stuck his head out of the door, and the fellow just took it off...

And so, it was the (this) "lawless West" into which "Johnny Two-Feathers" (as the Indians named him) made his beginnings. "I was the favorite of the whole family 'cause I was so bloomin' light-skinned and Dad always wanted a boy named Johnny," he recalled.

Yet many such children would later grow up to feel the difference in another way. As a young half-breed replied when asked his feelings of life on the reservation:

> You are a White Man. You have a place among your people. You count for something. Around us here are Indians; they revere their past, they have respect of their fellows. Here am I, neither an Indian nor a White Man...just nothing.

That stigma of "half-breed" never left him, and early in life he made a decision that even though he was light-complected, he would be all Indian inside. This would lead him into a complicated set of circumstances: to the White Man he must prove himself to be capable of being the one who always won. To the Red Man he must prove himself worthy of their highest traditions. And to prove himself to both sides, he must evolve into a different breed of man altogether, one who would master the art of self-reliance and virility to become something neither side could attain—a man's man. And to do this, he must first master the art of fighting.

Johnny's father had continued his police work off and on, and it was distressful to him to see where his young namesake was heading. The rest of the children were well-adjusted and doing well in school, but Johnny was fast establishing his reputation in his playground fights. This kind of fighting was more than just "schoolboy sparring." It consisted of biting, hair-pulling, and the use of knives and bricks. And the more he fought, the more taunted he became, inflaming his aggressiveness. It was not that he hadn't been taught differently:

> When we was little bitty kids, my mother, when it come to bedtime, we'd all have to get around and kneel and say our prayers, and when we come to one place that had a church, we had to go to Sunday school. They'd give us a few pennies, and everybody had to dress to go...

But Johnny never forgot his childhood confrontations. They would forge into him a creed and set of rules he would live by the rest of his life, and as a small boy he watched as white men made sport of the "ignorant savage":

> When the Indian came into town, he wasn't treated right at all. I remember at this store, some white men–they were laughing and trying to see if they could cheat a Cheyenne out of the few nickels he had. I didn't forget that, and for revenge, I sure gave away a lot of White Man's sheep when I herded for them later. I'd help the Indians pick out a good fat one...

Since he had decided to be "all Indian inside," he had also learned to see things from the Indian perspective, and he soon found himself suffering the same taunts:

> I fought because I thought it was part of the times. I was cussed out a time or two when I was a little kid, so I learned to fight. I would knock the living daylights out of any of 'em smaller and bigger than me. I whipped two in one day. I was going to school then. One was older and another was my age, but heavier. I hit the big one with part of a brick on the ankle. That knocked him out, then I got a hold of the other one and got my teeth into his hair until the teacher came out and broke it up. Then for no reason, these two kids—right in the middle of town—their grandfather put them onto me. I

was down by the livery barn where we hung out a lot, and they called me down. One of them had the rubber rim out of an old baby buggy stuck down his pants legs, and was goin' to work me over. That made me mad, and I fought 'em like crazy. But I think the reason the granddad put them onto me was because he had some crabapple trees we kids used to go down and help ourselves to; we didn't consider it stealing and I think he thought I was the ringleader.

In reality, he probably was.

This young, impressionable boy had found himself caught between two cultures. Indians had never considered food of any kind to be private property. They had scavenged for it for centuries. To call it "stealing" would have been proper for the White Man, but for Indians, it was game. He soon copied the Indian love of such diversions, and as he recalled:

Even in the worst of times it was always fun. Indians love pranks and jokes. There was this wagon that was loaded down with some logs, and they was on this hillside with it and some of the logs broke loose and rolled down the hill. They thought it was so funny that they turned the wagon over and pushed it down the hill too.

He laughed.

The reservation was his playpen, his circus, his fighting ring and shooting gallery all rolled into one. Nothing could tame him or hold him down; he was a free spirit, as detached from conventional thinking as the prairie tumbleweed. "I had too many mountains to climb–too many streams to fish," he mused. But there was a lot of loafing around the reservation Trading Post. Men who had once been busy on buffalo hunts now found themselves with little to do. And though encouraged to take up farming or cattle raising, they were having difficulty adjusting to a life of ration handouts and subsistence checks when they had (previously) spent their lives foraging and gathering food wherever they saw it. It was the Indian way. There had been times when rations stopped altogether, as Washington was pressured to force a new order: to make the "lazy Indian" work. But they could not leave the reservation without a permit, and on the occasions they did (for they were expected to provide at least two thirds of their food) nearly all the meat they "provided" was from the carcasses of buffalo killed by white hunters. Drinking, gambling, and petty thievery were now the only outlets to self-expression. Daily life held little incentive to those who could not let go of the past.

The Shoshones were fortunate in that Chief Washakie was their leader. He had always advocated coexistence with the white invader, and by his non-violent policy towards Washington, he had earned the respect and gratitude of President Grant. It had not been Washakie's policy toward other Indian tribes however, and once, during a fierce battle with the Crow at Crow Butte, he had killed the Crow chief, cut out his heart, ate part of it and skewered other portions on the end of a pole. He was not a wimp in any sense of the word, but showed a remarkable sensitivity and wisdom, reflected in his recorded reply when given a gift of a beautiful saddle by the President. He had been silent, showing no emotion whatsoever. Officials were puzzled, and pressed him to furnish some comment to be relayed to Washington. The proud and wise Chief uttered these words:

> When a favor is shown to a Frenchman, he feels it in his head, and his tongue speaks. When a kindness is shown to an Indian, he feels it in his heart; and the heart has no tongue.

Such words reflected the intellect of a scholarly sage, yet, as Johnny was to learn, there were inner traits among the Shoshones which revealed an impulsive, impatient and resentful nature. There was also the Indian way of dealing with life. The story was told that Washakie had been furious one day because his wife had removed her tent. She replied that her mother-in-law had persuaded her to move it to a safer place. The next day he was gone again, and when he returned, she had moved it a second time. Washakie picked up a rifle, rushed over to the tent of his mother-in-law and shot the woman dead! Thus were the violent times, the superstitions, the savage code of Indian justice molding an already sensitive outcast of a boy into a manhood which would only function in the seclusion and safety of the mountains. It could belong nowhere else, for after he learned of the Indian's fear of those towering peaks, it became the one thing, which if mastered and conquered, would earn him the respect and acceptance he so lacked:

> I learned everything by myself. Most of the Indians was afraid of the mountains, especially at that time. One of the Shoshones told me that when they come to that country there was these little people living in the mountains that had big chests, and I don't know, sometimes I believe they did. They said they killed them all off, but they figure they haunt them, and I think a whole lot works in your brain, because things happened to different Indians...

The Arapahoes had called them NIMERIGARS, or pigmies, and said they were of low mentality, small in stature, childlike and irresponsible. But they were also great fighters who used poisoned arrows and were cannibalistic. The Arapahoes also claimed they had killed them off by setting fire up a canyon where they had trapped them all.

Whether a tale of superstition or of fact, Johnny observed the saying:

> I knowed two Indian boys there real good. They were about my age. They were good swimmers too, and they thought they'd cross Bull Lake country. That was taboo for them for sure...

Bull Lake was an "enchanted" sheet of water sitting in a deep canyon. When the wind rushed through the gorge, it sounded like a buffalo bellowing. Near the water's edge was an enchanted rock with hieroglyphics. Any Indian who desired to become a medicine man was required to go to this lake, and if able to sleep there the whole night he would qualify. Most were overcome with fear:

> They crossed this little stream and it was pretty wild–should be just a little river. But they didn't make it; they both drowned.

Johnny continued:

> And when they found 'em, they was both laying along the bank. Their horses was right beside 'em. They couldn't get over the bank.

The mountains, then, became his obsession, his supreme goal. And from early boyhood he began learning the skills of the trapper and hunter, raiding the countryside like a hungry coyote:

> I used to trap way up the road. I had an old bicycle that you had to keep pumping. It didn't have any tires, so I run it on the rims. I remember going up there, and I'd catch muskrats and bring 'em home. I gotta lot of 'em. I went alone most of the time, but I had a little friend that lived way up there, and we sometimes caught muskrats together. Then I shot ducks. There was this cowman–a big shot. Out in his pasture across this creek (they called it Brush Creek), they had this pond. He didn't want nobody hunting on his place, but I went up there fishing one day and I saw this pond just covered with ducks. So boy, I just headed for home and got my dad's

shotgun—that kickin' thing—and I went down there and there was this fence with rails. I took aim from behind that fence and got a slather of ducks. I run down there real quick and gathered up them ducks and run back and got on the other side of the fence where I was safe, but the cowman's stepson—I seen him comin' with a big pistol in his hand—was sneaking up on me. But I made it back to this other man's property, so I just waved them ducks at him and said, "Ha-ha-ha!" Them ducks was good eating! So you see, I haven't been an angel all my life.

He laughed:

When I was 13, I'd be gone all summer, but I was all alone and quit school when I was 14. Me and Newton Ingram–he had a horse, a palomino called Pally, and I had a horse named Pete. We just fished and we'd go to sheep camps to get our meals. Most of them were really glad to see us–somebody to talk to. But I remember one time we went down, and we figured we'd live on fish. We went down this canyon and we fished and fished. We got so tired of eating fish and laying under just our saddle blankets that I remember Newt got so hungry he said, "Why is it God didn't make it so that we could eat grass like our horses?" He was so hungry!

Johnny was fast learning the survival skills that would become so essential in later years, but like most trappers and scouts, he learned it on his own, through the sometimes lonely days and nights wandering over the vast mountain ranges and into deep canyons:

> My folks tried their best to get me to get a job like everyone else, and so one day they got me this job with a construction company. The day I went to work everybody showed up to watch Johnny Luster work. Well, they had a wheelbarrow there, and they said I was to push that thing around all day. I looked at it, then turned around and headed for the mountains...

Here, he felt at home, a place which welcomed his awe and respect and offered it back from those in the valleys below who could not survive and conquer such wild and hostile places. Soon, they would all come to him for advice. They would come to him for the impossible task–for his wisdom and knowledge of the mountains. He would earn it from Indian and White Man alike and taste the pride of it all at winter's first snowfall as eager ears and envious hearts prodded him for stories of his adventures.

Thus was the beginning of Johnny Luster, the mountainman. And though he was still a youngster, mischievous and undisciplined, the days ahead would teach him many more painful lessons about life. He would learn something the wild animals already knew: that there was more to fear from man than anything in nature.

Several weeks had become months as I continued my sessions with Johnny, who seemed eager for our visits during the long winter days. His son, Johnny Jr., had dropped by. He was also a guide, as well as a successful businessman in Wasilla. They briefly discussed together some upcoming bear hunts as soon as spring arrived.

The two looked exactly alike, except for the apparent age difference and John, Jr.'s coal-black eyes and hair. I would want to interview him also at a later time.

The two men talked for a short while, then John Jr. left. "How many children do you have, Johnny?" I asked. "I got twelve. But you know what? If they hadn't brought in all these Vietnamese and Chinese, I woulda populated Alaska!" he laughed.

"And your wife? Is she still alive?"

"Which one?" he grinned. "I've had a dozen of them, too." That was a shock, but I didn't question him about it right then. I decided to sort it all out later. By now this old mountainman had thoroughly charmed me, and I was anxious for him to continue his amazing story.

*Johnny, Frank, and Paul Luster–Wind River Reservation,
Thanksgiving Day, 1938*

4
THE MAKING OF A RENEGADE

"For some, it was like having to watch their own death..."

Fortunately for "Johnny Two-Feathers," World War I came and went without him having to serve; he was too young. Years later, he would be too old for the Second, and the absence of this exposure to the outside world served to keep his wild, Indian nature intact. But there was too much excitement around Wind River country to give him any desire for distant horizons. There were far more possibilities right here, for he had discovered what he wanted out of life before he had shaved his first beard. He would hunt, and he would trap, and have a "ball" doing it and anything else that created the opportunity to prove himself "the best there was"–whether it was fighting, breaking horses, scouting or simply being the fastest runner on the reservation.

He and his younger brother Paul would years later drift into the guiding business in Wyoming, but for now these two, along with Newton Ingram, spent lazy summers immersed in their dream world...three "Huckleberry Finns" roaming their "Mississippi":

> I was drowning one time, and I counted the times I went under, me and this boy right along the road in this hole called Muddy Creek. It was deep, and there was this waterfall that made it a lot deeper. I thought I could swim, so I went in first and I started drowning. I kept going down, and I remembered they said when you went down the third time, you stayed. Well, I went down six times, but my brother Paul told me that the last time or two just the top of my head showed. He got to the edge of the drop off and throwed me the leg of my jeans and finally got me out and drug me onto the bank. By then I couldn't even raise an arm. Paul ran up the bank to try and get someone's attention, but he had forgotten he had taken off all his clothes to go swimming himself. He saw my sisters and some of their girlfriends and tried to flag them down, but as soon as they saw him standing there naked, they took off running.

He laughed, but he was lucky to be alive.

Days were filled with endless adventures, as Johnny scoured the countryside like a thirsty dog lapping up water. The area was still teeming with wild animals and was still a primitive wilderness with rutted wagon trails for roadways–the "Iron Horse" still the latest way to travel. But though the sun and seasons came and went with their same predictable cycles, there was a sense of being caught in the middle of inevitable change.

For some, it was like having to watch their own death, and old warriors felt the deep pain as, little by little, encroaching civilization ate away the unmarred landscape. It was to such men that the young "Johnny Two-Feathers" felt drawn to sit at their campfires and silently listen as these men recounted the old days. Many were survivors of famous battles and were counted as heroes by the young boys. For the most part, they were the only ones who cared to hear the Indian version of historic events, or to savor their peculiar wisdom.

"When White Man and Indian walk side by side, they do not see alike," old warriors would recount. For Johnny, such a saying would have significance throughout his life, for the two sides were bred inside of him and were often at odds with one another. "Look at this fire. The White Man builds a big fire and sits far off from it. The Indian makes a little fire and sits close," an aging brave would continue, reinforcing the differences which only wise and spiritual men would perceive.

Such words were like meat, meant to be chewed and relished, and never forgotten. As he grew older, Johnny could see that both the White Man and the Indian were losing valuable knowledge as time eliminated these survivors. His mind became a logbook, a diary of such fragments:

When I go back down to visit the reservation, they act like I'm some kind of big-shot because they want to know about the old ways and most everybody's died off that knew about those things. They had wanted me to show them where the old burial ground was, 'cause things are changing now–where they've got the right to respect their own dead. So I showed it to 'em. Since my time down there, it had become pretty well growed up in some rocks and people have been desecrating them graves. I once saw a kid, fifteen or sixteen, take his knife and whack off some copper bracelets off a corpse. That wasn't right. I couldn't have them in my house! Indians are just as much human as the rest of 'em, but to this day they're looked down on.

The Battle of Little Big Horn would never be forgotten by either side. Though the Shoshones had only acted as scouts and not participated in the massacre, the Arapahoes and Sioux had not forgotten their victory there and passed on, by word of mouth, their side of the story–a version not exactly matching the White Man's. Johnny recalled:

The Sioux have a joke. They say they're the ones who "Siouxed" Custer. The Arapahoes told me that they went out and tied buffalo grass together so the soldiers' horses would trip when they broke for it. One old Indian told me that Custer was not killed on that hill like they said he was, but was killed while he was crossing the river and soldiers ran up on each side of

him and took him across. When they was bat-
tling, there was another soldier who broke and
went away from all the rest, trying to escape.
But he crossed the river and for some reason
turned his horse around and sat for a minute,
then killed himself. Two years ago there was
this fire that went through that battlefield and
burnt off the grass, and by golly if they didn't
find that soldier's bones and stuff. I don't know
why he did it; if it had been me I'da kept going...

Because of his extraordinary knowledge of the
Indian tales, Johnny would, in his old age, be called
upon by many historians and archaeologists to assist
in the search for past relics:

When I go back down to the reservation next
time, I'm gonna show them this sinkhole where
there's been a lot of stuff taken off Custer's soldiers and throwed in there. The Arapahoes decided they better not bring it in, so they threw it
in that sink hole. It could be the place, 'cause
there's some juniper poles throwed across it,
and juniper never rots...

I could detect his pride in knowing things others
had forgotten. Was it all mountain man stories, or was
he actually a fragile link between past and present? The
evidence proved his memory was startling:

Chief Foster down in Wyoming is getting married to old Chief Washikee's great-granddaugh-
ter. All the old Indians, all the old white ones–

it's funny how they all just up and died, so the next generation's took over, and they don't know nothing about where it is. They don't even know where the Shoshone campground was in the warring days. I told them it was up in Little Muddy Basin. Well, they went up there but they couldn't find it. So I said, "I'll go up there with you." I looked for a tree that stuck out on both sides. It was a pinon tree, and there was big sheep horns in it. I've been up there so many times. I told 'em it was in that tree, but you have to cut off the top of it and peal it back to the horns. Well, I went up there, and stopped when I found it and he said, "Where?" And I said, "You're standing right on 'em. Get out there and see those tipi rings, one right after the other," and there was hundreds of 'em.

It was the Shoshone campground!

Few men could match the skills of observation that had been developed in Johnny from childhood. His senses were fine-tuned and honed to a critical sharpness, so essential to this emerging mountainman, hunter and guide. Every rock, every tree, was a landmark:

They wanted me to find some breastworks for them up in some cliffs where they had some rocks piled up. The Indians used to go behind them to shoot. I showed 'em where the buffalo jump was; it was a hole on this white ledge. My brother actually found it, and over the years it's been covered. But in this hole my brother found a gun and some old soldier boots. Lots of stuff out of there...

The adventures would never end, but it was difficult for Johnny's parents to see their growing son dropping out of school and running, rebelliously, into every avenue that promised excitement and fun. Why wasn't he like the rest of his brothers? Why didn't he settle down and find himself?

The answer to that would be a complex one. While still in his teens, Johnny (in spite of his wildness) had discovered within himself the ability to survive in the rawness of nature, something that set him apart from other boys and even men. It would be his "medal of honor," his source of pride. Whether at that point in time anyone appreciated this accomplishment, it was (nonetheless) an achievement and goal which separated him from everyone else.

The older boys took up professions and went their ways. Paul loved being with Johnny on his forays, but since he was younger and still in school, he could only be with him during the summer months. This left Johnny to roam at will among his Indian friends, sheepherders and an assortment of unsavory specialists in mischief.

The Depression years brought many changes to the lives of most Americans, some of them devastating. The stock market crash and the collapse of the banking system had paralyzed the nation, giving rise to a poverty never before experienced by its 40 million inhabitants. But for the Lusters and the Wind River

Reservation Indians, they could not have been in a better place to weather the storm. Those times barely made any difference at all, for they were already used to hardship and living off the land. There was always plenty to eat, what with the abundant produce available in the valley, livestock on the ranches and wildlife in the mountains. Johnny soon found himself in "business":

> I had a rifle and lots of shells. For a whole elk I could get ten dollars. Furs weren't worth much then, usually only five dollars, no matter what it was. I trapped for marten and fox a little, but later fox got to where they weren't worth nothing and that's when I went to working for the Indian Department–trapping for them. I made my money that way. Then one day a circus carnival came to town and the "fat lady" and some of 'em wanted me to show 'em where to fish, so I found out then I could make some money guiding.

There were also vast sheep herds that needed tending up in the meadows, and he had already formed close ties to the sheepherders, who had always welcomed the little "mountain boy" into their camps. As long as Johnny was busy in the mountains, he would stay out of trouble. But the lean times often necessitated his finding work in the valley:

> I broke horses for people at $10 a horse. Nowadays it's $150, but if you could turn two horses, even at $10 a head, in them days that was a lot

of money. 'Course you took a chance on breaking your neck.

He laughed:

I've been whopped in my chin fighting, but the only thing that ever broke my jaw was an old stallion. His foot was too big!

But his skill with horses would play a big factor in things to come...

5
THE OUTLAW YEARS

"It was just the times we lived in..."

While still in his teens, Johnny discovered another diversion–stealing horses:

I got messed up by being young and mouthy, and I got into the wrong side of the law by playing "Indian" with the Indian boys and the horses. It was during the cowmen trouble, which gave the Indians an opening; they began stealing horses. You have to understand, stealing horses was the Indians' game. It was a kind of honor, and they didn't see anything wrong with it at all. Most of the people didn't give a darn. They would ship those horses to the slaughter house anyway in later years. I knew one guy, I took his horse and broke it good and used it, and the old guy knew I was using it. Finally, I came and turned it into his pasture and the old guy saw it and said, "I guess Johnny is through with the horse for this year, so I'll take him home." It

73

was broke, so that tickled him to death.

But it was a lot more serious than that. Johnny had met up with the notorious "Cheyenne Charlie" at a place called Dirty Ole's close to Black Mountain. They decided to hang out together up in the mountains, hunting and trapping and running horses over the mountains into Cody. To Cheyenne Charlie it was a way of life; to Johnny it was fun. After getting a trapping permit from a rancher named Foster Scott, they entered the DuBois Badlands.

"It was nothing but wild!" as Johnny described it. Indeed it was. The trail into Cody would cross the mountains and rendezvous at Wiggins Fork and Bear Creek, so desolate and wild a place that it is still largely uninhabited:

> We throwed in together and went to trapping, setting traps as high as 11,000 feet. One time, at Togwotee Pass, we was coming through there, and this fellow had deserted his wife and baby— a 5 or 6 year-old girl—and she was freezing to death. The snow was blowing and the wind...it was cold! So I wrapped the baby in my coat and put it in my arms, but there was no saving her, she died and we buried her out there. So we took her mother out, but we had to keep on the move...

Dirty Ole's was a sort of rendezvous place for Johnny to meet his family and friends, but it was nothing more than a filthy cabin with a dirt floor:

Dirty Ole had skinned out an old dog of his that had died and made him into a sort of rug. Me and Cheyenne Charlie would stop there to clean up, and one time when we did, Dirty Ole said he'd just clean up, too. That surprised us. Well, he took off all his clothes, and his underwear was so filthy it stuck to his skin! Dirty? This guy was so lazy he wouldn't even empty the ashes out of the cook stove until he just had to; they were all over the floor! I thought about getting some gunpowder and putting it in those ashes and giving him a real surprise, but I didn't.

He laughed:

I did, however, put one over on both of them. Ole loved horses, and one time the two of them was really hungry for some meat. I went and killed a colt and gave 'em both a hindquarter. They said to me, "Boy, that sure was great elk meat!" They'd of killed me if they'd known that was horsemeat.

Keeping his horse-stealing ventures secret, Johnny went back down to the reservation to sell his furs and got a job herding cattle at the Shotgun Ranch. But there was more to that than appeared. There was a fight going on, and the ranch owner had a young daughter named Jan. And Johnny was interested in both:

I was driving cattle, helping her dad, because they were trying to run him out. He was an ornery old bugger. Why, that little guy would fight a buzz saw. They all had to pick on him on account of his temper. 'Course they all had tempers, too. But anything he did, he was trying to get this school going at the Shotgun Ranch on the reservation, and he took an awful beating to get it. Two big guys got a hold of him one night when they were holding a meeting there and beat the livin' daylights out of him. They really beat him up badly. He was in bed over it. And they got to jumping on me. I'm about 5'5", but some of them got a hold of me and I took some awful beatings, too. Sometimes two guys would hold me and another beat on me, but if I could, I'd learned a long time ago to grab hold and hang on and wear 'em down...

Frontier justice was still a matter of personal interpretation to a lot of people, even at this point in time. Not all "lawmen" were honorable, but served the interests of the wealthy cattlemen who were determined to overrun the smaller outfits. The reservations had their own laws and policemen, and whatever authority or warrants were binding in other areas stopped at reservation boundary lines. It was an indescribable mess. The old ways had not yet died out, neither for the Indian nor for the white vigilantes. Because of his impetuous and easily-provoked ways, Johnny had become a thorn in the sides of certain men–a "half-breed" shrimp who needed to be eliminated, and they were looking for any excuse to do it. When he returned to the mountains and his "other" activity, Johnny soon gave them the excuse they were looking for:

My big mouth got me into trouble. Cheyenne had met up with a Roy Turbell, a soldier from the first war who had tried farming, but he was always sick and had a lot of troubles. When Cheyenne found him, Roy was short on food, so Cheyenne went and stole a cow from this man and hung and quartered it for him. Well, the owner of that cow came by to bum a meal off Roy, and they had told him it was elk meat. But he soon figured it out and notified the authorities. Well, I came by a few days later, and when they told me about it I said, "Well, just tell 'em I did it!" I made a bad mistake, just being a smart-aleck. Roy knew the truth, but he wouldn't speak up. And Cheyenne was already on the run.

The law was now hot on Johnny's heels. A bounty was placed on his head:

I was on the run for sure now. They was all after me for helping Jan's dad, and them cowmen was fighting about nothing. One of them was beating up this little guy 'cause he married the woman he wanted to marry. And another was a killin' outfit, even the sheriff. He'd killed people who didn't pay up their protection money; so he thought I was a real prize if he could bring me in.

Johnny headed for the mountains and the Badlands, the posse on his heels. They would soon discover that this youngster was playing in his ballpark, and that his years of roaming the high country had taught him tricks they had never thought about. They followed him for hours, tracking him into the snow line where they picked up snowshoe imprints going a certain direction, only to find out he had put the snowshoes on backward to fool them. To keep moving in the cold, he set fire to rabbit bushes which quickly ignited and offered him momentary warmth. When they finally caught onto what he was doing, he would set fires on one side of the mountain and quickly vanish in another direction.

But it was not all mountainman skills that helped him evade his captors. Once, when sleeping in a dugout on Steamboat Mountain, he had a dream in which these men came and were stabbing him to death. He took it as a warning they were out to kill him (which they were), and left the dugout and climbed up a tall fir tree. He hadn't been there long when the posse came and spent the night camped under that very tree! For some months Johnny managed to evade his captors; it was a hard life, being on the run. But there were quite a few men running from the law at that time who became Johnny's companions:

> I shoulda picked up a good string of horses and headed for Alaska. There was other mountains besides those in Wyoming. I talked to some of the others out there in the Badlands. One was Grant Metzer. He said he had got into it with a couple of bankers down in Oklahoma and shot 'em both, and he made it as far as Wyoming

and saw the mountains and figured he better stop here. He raised a family and made it. And then there was this guy named Adams. He had an arm shot off by the law, swimming the Red River trying to get away. He carried a pistol for a long time. I knew a lot of those old people. I had to survive with them. When I needed to take some furs down, somebody would meet me. I'd head for Dirty Ole's. But they found out about it and came hot on my heels. Dirty Ole gave me this real skinny old horse with no saddle and I took off, riding him bareback. I had some frozen marten on my back, and that old horse was so bony his backbone was like a saw. I guess that's why my legs is so short, they got sawed off on that animal when I high-tailed it out of there.

He laughed:

When I got down the side of the mountain, lo and behold there was my brother in an old Studebaker at the fork of the road, just waiting for me. He took me over to these other folks' house, and they had this real large Indian woman named Bessie. She got in the car with us and they drove me back towards the reservation where I was safe. As they drove up, there was that sheriff Jimmy Thompson. So she threw her coat over me and kinda sat on me and they just drove by him and waved "hi" and got through. Everyone was hiding me.

But Johnny was finally caught, and sentenced to prison in Rawlings. He would be there for almost a year. Those long months behind bars were his first experiences with confinement of any type–almost unbearable for a young man who had always anticipated the thrills of hunting and trapping seasons. It was a frightful lesson he would never forget and never wanted to repeat again. He was ashamed of himself and the trouble he had brought to his family. Cheyenne Charlie finally moved on, and Johnny returned to the Wind River area after he had served his time. But he remained friends with this "scrapper" (as Johnny called him) for years:

> I killed a lot of people, but never murdered anyone. It was just the times we lived in; it was all wild then. After the Dust Bowl days started bringing in the Nebraskans, things changed. They intermarried with everybody and kinda settled things down. Back in the old days, if even a fist fight broke out, everybody got involved. But even up here in Alaska, three different times I was brought to court and people would try to bring up my past, and three judges all said, "That was war, and I don't want to hear anymore about it..."

Johnny had indeed been lucky. Rawlings' prison has since become a historical site not for its beauty, but for its notorious history as one of the most brutal and murderous institutions ever built. Few who ever went there returned alive...

6
THE DUST SETTLES

"...the mountains were a jealous lover that could lay traps in the valleys, just as he lay them in the hills..."

After returning to the reservation, Johnny was still young, barely twenty, but much wiser. However, he still had no desire to change his routine. For the rest of his life, he would continue the hunting and trapping seasons, and whatever fell in between might consist of anything. There was always horse-breaking to do, herding cattle at the Shotgun Ranch or sheep herding up in the high meadows. As much as possible, he kept a "low profile" and stayed in the mountains, sometimes for over a year.

In the spring of 1930, Johnny came off the high country with his pelts and headed for the reservation. Summer was coming up–another lull. But that particular year would introduce some changes for him he would remember all his life.

At the same time Johnny was maturing, Hollywood had also come of age, from the silent era into serious epics. The word "movies" sparked everyone's imagination in those days—a certain release from depression, worries, and boredom.

The love affair had begun with the rise of the movie idol, whose good looks and fabricated image made him or her household words and began to dictate the fashions and tastes of America. Nothing was in more demand than the "B" Western. It was a spin-off from the "Buffalo Bill" extravaganzas that had excited Madison Square Garden and other amphitheaters years earlier, when cowboys and Indians staged authentic battles and old worn-out chiefs, such as Sitting Bull, had been on display like sideshow freaks. Everyone was taken in with an especially insatiable thirst for the cowboy movie idol. Tom Mix, Tim McCoy and others were Saturday-night fare for most of the country, and America's infatuation with the Western was only beginning.

Fox Studio director, Raoul Walsh, had been looking for a star for his $3 million-dollar spectacular "The Big Trail." It would have all the ingredients: wagon trains, cattle drives, Indian attacks—the works. It would originate in New Mexico and finish up near Jackson Hole, Wyoming. He had decided to gamble with a young man named Marion Michael, who had acted in brief walk-on parts in other movies, but was now working in the prop department. His tall, rugged looks and natural ability drew Walsh's one good eye (he wore an eye patch), but the name would have to go. From now on, Marion Michael would be John Wayne.

That spring, the crew moved into Jackson Hole, and Walsh sent word into the reservations that he needed some Indians to work as extras. Johnny recalled:

> The pay was $4 a day and board–a fortune in those days. They come into town looking for Indians. My brother Paul woke me up and said, "Get up quick! We got a good paying job. We're gonna be warriors in this movie," ...him and I.

Soon, a large bus drove onto the reservation, plowing up a cloud of dust behind its wheels. The excited Indians scrambled aboard as Johnny and Paul rushed for a seat for the long ride to Jackson Hole. Many of them had never seen a movie before, yet this was an event of indescribable importance and good fortune, and they knew it. It would be fun, just being themselves. There would be lots of action, something tailor-made for Johnny. He was not aware of it then, but his skill with horses and love of pranks would lead him into a lifetime friendship with this new actor, John Wayne:

> The way I met John was because I raised so much pranks. This old Raoul Walsh–I just couldn't resist it, because they had these big towers built and he'd get up there and holler at us through that big horn thing, and tell us Indians what to do. Well, I got enough of it one day and I hollered back at him, "Yes, Ma'am!" When I found out it bothered him, then I just kept it up. Oh, I tell you...he was just so mad! He'd send out some guys to find out who had

said it, but the Indians wouldn't tell on me. That's one good thing about the Indians, one won't tell on another. So, John came over and got acquainted, and boy, he thought I was all right 'cause I knew how to ride anything they had there bareback or anyway they wanted me to ride, and we kinda spoke the same language.

The whole affair was fun for Johnny:

I was riding a horse, naked except for a breech cloth. At noontime we'd all line up behind one another to go pick up our lunch and some of the Arapahoes hung back. They had been waiting for me to make a run for the lunch wagon, and just as I did, they grabbed my breech cloth and there I was–stark naked! Well, I didn't know anything else to do but turn around and grab it, and I ran behind a big old Arapahoe, put both arms around him and hung on! I made sure they couldn't get me loose until I put my breech cloth back on. We was always having pranks like that.

He chuckled:

But John Wayne was for real. While we was doing that picture, when we charged the wagons I seen him grab this girl. We was getting those white people right and left there, and he got her behind his saddle and galloped around and found an opening in the wagon train and jumped inside the circle. They hadn't planned it that way at all, but they got it all on film.

When we slacked off and was standing around, everybody was congratulating him because he figured out something quick to make it really look good. I just made one movie with John, and another with Tim McCoy, but me and John wrote to one another for years.

He added:

John offered to help me get a job in the movies after he got to be a big shot, but I saw those guys sure paid a price for having a lot of money and things. (Meaning they gave up their free-dom–something Johnny could never do!)

After his stint in the movies, Johnny went back to the reservation and got a job herding cattle at the Shot-gun Ranch. And that summer Johnny's interests sud-denly changed: he fell in love.

He had known Jan all his life, even gone to school with her as kids. But days of sharing the range chores had blossomed into romance and a decision to make her his wife.

The school they had earlier fought for was still in operation, and as Johnny passed by it every day. He had no idea it would turn out that he had taken all those beatings for his school. Jan's mother was the school teacher and she was teaching the kids there in their home:

The old man, why, he figured, "Well, there's that kid; I'll get a lot of work out of him now."

But his wife cornered me one day and said, "Did you go to school?" I said, "No, I don't go to school." She said, "Well, you're going to school now!" So she pulled me off everyday and I went to school. 'Course in-between times, Jan and I herded cattle.

Women in Wyoming were pretty much independent and liberated; most of the ranch girls shared the chores with the men. It would be the first state to give women the right to vote, and women's suffrage movements used Wyoming as their genesis. Johnny would find this out for himself:

Jan's name was really Clara Jane, but she changed it because she said it always reminded her of that cow picture of Clara the Cow. She's hardboiled. Boy, a horse throwed me off one time, and she said, "Smart-aleck!"–just because I was trying to show her what I could do. I was on my horse and I hung onto the horn and reached away down and touched the horse on the nose with a piece of bread which was part of my lunch, and the horse went up in the air and when he come down I was about halfway on the horse and halfway off. He just throwed me out onto the salt sage, and she just kept on saying, "Smart-aleck! Smart-aleck!" But she was a good scout.

It would take more than that to keep these two rebels together.

About two years later, Johnny's father died and was buried near Riverton. Johnny remembers:

> He was an old man, all dried up, so really nobody knew just how old he was. I was with him when he died. It was in the wintertime, and a big blizzard had hit the reservation. No one was moving about the morning he died. I shot a horse. I just had that "Indian feeling" when I killed the horse. I had to; he woulda just laid there, so finally I just went out and killed him.

What Johnny was referring to was the Indian custom of killing the horse belonging to the dead man–a way of releasing the bond between man and animal so they could be together in the happy hunting ground.

Most Indians mourned their losses for days, even weeks; some slashing themselves with knives, venting their grief. In the graveyards were placed personal possessions of the deceased. Their final resting places were often covered over with their iron bedsteads.

As the Luster family huddled together that cold, winter day there were many thoughts going through Johnny's mind–his Dad's jet black eyes and his calm, deliberate manners...a man who had tasted this land's primeval beauty as a youngster, learning to love it passionately...an inherited trait passed down from his father and Johnny's grandfather–William Luster. A love that even the tragedy of Civil War could not wipe out. "What if he had not come back?"

The thought was too frightful to think about, especially for Johnny. The mountains were all he had or ever wanted to have. How could he live without seeing the flocks of geese and ducks returning to thawing lakes, or hearing the bellows of rutting bulls in the elk herds or feeling the crunch of snow along the trap lines?

Yet, for some reason, he seemed to be the only one in the family with such a passionate determination to spend his life there. How could they be expected to understand his failure to become "civilized" like the rest of them, when he did not understand it himself? Was he some kind of throwback to his grandfather, who had stayed in this country to fish, trap and hunt with the Indians almost a century earlier? Was he—in some mysterious way—taking up where his grandfather left off, fulfilling his life two generations later?

He had never fit in, and it seemed as if the valley floor contained something that aroused within him the worst of himself. Was it the spirits of mischief and cruelty, the violent demons of hatred and murder which overwhelmed him, or was it simply that he could never think of himself as anything but one of those mountain men and had been purposed to be one? He thought on the times his father had counseled him, trying to instill his own sense of honor and cool-headed wisdom into this "favorite" of his, all for naught. But he could never be the farmer his father had become nor go the same path of his brothers. For some reason, though he did try to do right, it just never turned out that way for him.

He and Jan and the two babies (by this time Sue and Nancy had been born) went back into the mountains to continue the trapping season. It got to be a way of life Johnny wanted to last forever; making the mountains home half the year, then back down to the reservation and the Shotgun Ranch. It would take him a long time to finally conclude that he could never divide his life that way–that the mountains were a jealous lover which could lay traps in the valleys, just as he lay them in the hills:

> I trapped, and lived mostly in cabins. You could fix up a camp real quick, 'cause it didn't take long. I'd go down a few miles to get a load of lumber and fix it up really good.

Johnny reflected on those times and the changes of modern ways:

> That's what's the matter with people now; they get some land away out, and they can't do nothing about it 'cause it's so far out they can't get no building material in. Used to, two or three of 'em would get together and they had a log house up in a week, and everybody was happy, and it was good and warm. Then, everybody was happy. The women all seemed so good and happy then. They'd all get together and be a-chattering. It didn't take' em long to put up a log outfit.

Johnny and Jan found their life in the mountains exciting and exhilarating. Together they savored the

91

sounds of wildlife and the groanings of nature, ever learning the lessons of adjustment to its whims. During one early morning, Johnny looked up at the peaks of Washitee Needles. He could see that the sun was further north now, and days were getting longer. He would soon have to pack out their furs and trapping season would be over for another year. As late evening approached, the dogs began barking excitedly. The thud of rocks echoed from a small clearing.

Jan suddenly yelled, "Look! There's a bear!"

Johnny turned to see an enormous grizzly turning up rocks. Just then the animal heard the dogs and wheeled around, his huge frame standing upright in a show of ferocious power. Johnny quickly grabbed his rifle, a little .25-35.

"Could it possibly kill such an animal?" he agonized.

"I took a crack at him, and he just jumped and then stood still," he remarked.

There would not be a chance for them to escape him if he didn't fall soon. Johnny fired a second shot. This time the bullet tore through the monster's heart, knocking him off his feet as he tumbled over the rocks and fell into a heap of brown fur. They waited, breathlessly, for him to show signs of life, and began to pelt him with rocks. Johnny yelled for the dogs, who circled the animal, nipping at him with cautious assault. But it was over; the bear was dead:

We gutted him out and tied him up; it was getting so late. Then we went on down to camp. We found out later they had a reward out on that bear. He was a big one!

Thus Johnny killed his first bear, the first among many he would encounter during his lifetime.

I asked him if he was scared. "I get nervous about facing people sometimes, but the other things—I got that whipped!" he answered.

He failed to mention what Jan thought.

7
A WIND FROM THE NORTH

"It offered itself as a beautiful virgin bride..."

Several thousand miles northwest of Wind River, events were taking place which would have a profound effect upon Johnny's future. There were shifts in the wind, and it was blowing–not only upon the Midwest farms, but as far away as Alaska.

The giant snake of Rocky Mountains jutted its way across Western Canada into the Yukon Territory, making its one last statement in the huge Alaska Range. Purchased from Russia in 1867, (six years after Johnny's grandfather had died in the Civil War) Alaska was still a territory, as wild and untamed a place as one could imagine. Yet it was the logical next and last step in the long history of the American homesteader who had leaped, jump-frog style, from the Eastern shores, across the Alleghenies, into the Rockies and on to Oregon. There was no place else to go, and if it had not been for a series of events, it would have remained largely un-inhabited except for the Natives and Indians and some resolute sourdoughs until military forces arrived at the start of World War II.

But scattered across Nebraska, Minnesota, and Kansas were thousands of farmers, mostly immigrants, who had been dealt the twin blow of depression and devastation. The farm belt had been hard hit, and Washington would listen to any suggestion as to what to do about it.

Agricultural experts and social workers were convinced that Alaska might be a solution, especially a small area known as the Matanuska Valley, located some forty miles east of Anchorage. Though the growing season was short, crops grew rapidly in the long daylight hours.

"The Colony Project," as it was called, was designed not only to offer a new start to these stricken farmers, but hopefully to lead others to venture north, assuring this "last frontier" of settlement. Elaborate plans were drawn up to transport, feed, and house some 200 families chosen from the thousands of farmers who applied. They would be settled into a particularly beautiful valley located at the base of a jagged peak later to be named "Pioneer Mountain." It was completely isolated, except for a railroad line into Anchorage, and consisted of a small village called Palmer.

The colonists would be allotted some 8,000 acres for crops, and another 18,000 acres for grazing land. It looked like a dream come true. But Alaska was not Oregon, and for the most part, the Colony Project was an exercise in futility and proved to be a bureaucratic nightmare. No one seemed to be foresighted enough to ask where or to whom these farmers were to sell their produce–if they managed to get a crop during the brief growing season, which was often nothing but continual rain. The Territory, at that time, had only seven towns with over one thousand people. Harsh winters, shipping costs, and isolation would sour this experiment and doom it to near failure. Had it not been for the establishment of military bases which gladly bought what produce was available and offered jobs to the disillusioned farmers, most of the colonizers would have left by 1940.

In spite of the colony mess, Alaska did have a mystique that was rapidly vanishing from the American West. It offered itself as a beautiful virgin bride to those rugged individualists who, with foresight and tenacious courage, stuck it out and remained to call it "home." The reward would be a love affair from the beginning, and those stricken with it found the rest of the world pale in comparison. They did not know it at the time, but they were birthing anew—in their generation—the last vestige and seed of the American Pioneer. It would either live or die on the banks of the Susitna, the Nenana, the Yukon, or on the slopes of the Wrangells, the Talkeetnas, or the Kuskokwim. They would weather the storm, the uncertainties, the days of boom and the days of bust, because they had already found their "El Dorado" in Alaska itself. They could only hope that part of them would survive to love it in the same way.

It might be difficult to know what thoughts were going through the minds of these early sourdoughs as they watched the colony bustle with the wide-eyed immigrants. But Alaska was a big land, with opportunity for all. And if a man did not make it in his profession or skill, there were always other ventures.

Jimmy Simpson had come to Alaska around 1913 from Wyoming. Professionally, he had a law degree, like others in his family. Nephew to the then-governor of Wyoming, Milred Simpson, he could have advanced himself politically, for Wyoming was a sparsely settled state with his family already an accepted dynasty. But Jimmy hated the confining walls of legal offices and was looking for other pursuits. An avid big-game hunter, he knew all too well what an untapped bonanza lay at his doorstep.

Until 1904, there had been little exploration of the country north of Cook Inlet, nor did the Matanuska colonists care to explore the towering Alaska Range. The limited hunting that did occur was mainly for subsistence and had been practiced for centuries by native Indians and Eskimos. Alaska had not been invaded by wealthy "safari" types who hunted for wall trophies and bragging rights.

There was, as yet, no easy way to get there. Hunters could only drool at the stories of vast caribou herds, mammoth Kodiak bear, Kenai moose and Dall sheep locked into a wilderness of 586,000 square miles. But August of 1920 marked a significant change to all of that. On that day, four DeHaviland Liberty planes flew over Alaskan soil enroute to Nome from the Atlantic Coast and landed at Wrangell. It was the first time an airplane had ever been seen in the territory, and signaled the exciting promise of mail and passenger service from the lower states. Now it would be possible to bring the wealthy Eastern hunters into the state, and Jimmy Simpson was elated. The guiding business could be quite a financial bonanza if someone had the proper contacts with rich customers, something he did have. Men would pay plenty for VIP treatment, first-class service and good guides–not those "run-of-the-mill" types who knew little more than their clients.

To prove his resolve, this lawyer-turned-guide would lead his customers into the raw wilderness dressed impeccably in a business suit–quite a ridiculous sight to the weathered trappers and sourdoughs hired to pack them in. Nevertheless, his venture paid off, and he soon had one of the premier hunting outfits in the Territory. It would attract a steady clientele until interrupted by the Second World War.

Back in Wyoming, Johnny had also felt a lot of changes. His marriage to Jan had fallen apart, as would all his relationships with women. For in spite of his apparent success in the woods, Johnny's personal life was not all that idyllic; family responsibilities produced certain infringements into his lifestyle. Jan could not always accompany him on his long forays, and with children, it was disruptive and demanding.

It was an arrangement that would put a strain on any marriage, for few women could be content with a "wild and crazy man" who took off hunting for six months to a year at a time, was always in trouble of some kind and could never be a father or husband with any regularity. Yet, it was all he knew and lived for.

Women to Johnny were either "good scouts" or "hard-boiled hellcats," yet he was never single for very long, even after he and Jan went separate ways. It was a fact that Johnny could never come to terms with. The days of the squaw wife and her mountainman were a thing of the past. He would joke:

> Wives? I've had a dozen of 'em. I was on the mountain one time and I thought, what the heck, I'll just go down and marry 'em all! I knowed this real nice French-Canadian girl, she was the best of the whole lot, but she was Catholic, and we got married in the Catholic church by the priest. Everything was okay. Then one day, that priest said to her, "You're not married to him, he's been married before!" But they didn't know how that marriage was–there's no record of it. Then she went back to New Hampshire and the priest back there he said, "That's a bunch of baloney." He said she was married to me. So her brother came back to find me, but they found out I done went and got another one. So that did that...

He could simply not bother himself with the formalities and entanglements of acceptable family life. His son John, Jr. explains:

I'm sure he just said, "Heck for divorces." He just declared himself divorced. It was the Indian way. He would fall for a lady, and then go back into the mountains. The women would feel locked in and you couldn't blame them for it.

It was, despite his Caucasian roots, the Indian nature that prevailed, whether instinctively or purposely. For the Shoshones, there was no special marriage ceremony, and women did all the work while the men hunted and trapped–the children left as free spirits to roam at will.

After Jan, he had married a Minnie, then a Stella, a Lillie, a Francis, and then remarried Jan (though they soon lived apart).

"There coulda' been two or three more wives in there," John, Jr. added.

But circumstances were forcing Johnny to think seriously at settling down to a more ordered lifestyle. Federal regulations were now restricting the taking of big game, for it was a sobering fact that without some sort of management, all of the animals would go the way of the buffalo and there would be nothing left at all. No one knew that better than Johnny Luster, but it was also a painful reality to experience fate's callous blow upon his freedom to do as he pleased–whenever and wherever he wanted to do it. The days of men and women heading west in railcars, shooting anything that moved without any restraint or control were long gone, nor was the self-styled mountainman free to roam and subsist ungoverned. He, like Jimmy Simpson, would have to get into the guiding business.

With a string of pack horses, a guide license, and lots of experience, Johnny soon had a growing reputation quite different from the one he had cultivated earlier. Most men already recognized that without question, Johnny Luster knew the Wyoming mountains better than any man alive. Every game trail, every bull elk, every bear den was mapped out in his brain–a virtual walking log book of their mannerisms, habits and peculiarities. Word got around about the Wyoming mountainman. There would be no need for advertising. Many inquiries would come to Riverton simply addressed: "Johnny-Two-Feathers." Hunters were eager for elk especially, and he kept busy every minute of the hunting season.

But the lulls between hunting and trapping seasons made him restless and lonely, and during one such period, Johnny wandered down into Kansas. It was there that he met Lillie:

> What was I doing down there? Oh, I was just running around, nothing to do. There was no hills there, nothing, just mud. I went down on a train. It didn't take me long to get acquainted with somebody, and I met Lillie. She was half Cherokee, so I figured she'd make a good scout. We got married and went back to Wyoming.

The pattern had now repeated itself for the fourth time, but Lillie would remain with him longer than all the others, despite their stormy marriage.

In 1937, Johnny took Vern Cunningham and his family on their first big game hunt. His wife, Hilda, now 92 years old, still remembers that event:

> We were over on Bear Creek and Johnny was packing in some hunters and he had to have the horses, so he left us women behind. It was bitter cold, so we slept in the "wickiup," which was pine poles around a large tree, the top covered with pine bows for the roof. He left his dog, Tux, with us. Old Tux kept my feet warm, as he was inside with us. The next morning we went up on the mountain, and there was a big cave up there with pine poles in the front of it. They called them "slicks," and they were where they would get wild horses and put them in this big cave. (Perhaps also used to hide stolen horses.)
>
> When the men returned with a wagon, we left Sacajawea Lodge, and as the day wore on and we got higher up, we left the wagon and took the horses. Finally, we all had to walk. We camped at a beautiful lake, and the men left us and went to another lake to fish. While they were gone, a big bear came to pay us a visit. He passed up the panyards (boxes used to store supplies which were slung over pack animals) that had food in them and stood up on his hind legs. He sure was mad! I asked Lillie if there was a gun in camp. She had a little gun of some sort, so I got it and kept shooting towards the bear, and

he finally left.

That was quite an experience for the women, and Johnny didn't forget Hilda's efforts to kill the bear. Later, up on Bear Creek, a grizzly broke into Johnny's corral while he was tending to the horses. With nothing but an axe with him, Johnny swung at the charging animal and hit him in the head, stunning his senses. Before he could focus his eyes well, Johnny took aim and buried the axe into his skull with one blow, cutting his head in half. Hilda remembers:

> He brought the hide down to town and wanted me to have it. There was a split in the hide where he had hit the bear with the axe. We laughed when I asked him what to do when one comes charging.
>
> He replied, "Don't try shaking hands with him, he might decide to slap you!"

Typical Johnny Luster.

Lillie quickly bore him three daughters, which were to accompany their parents into the woods as soon as they were born. Johnny had, by now, fathered a total of seven children: five girls and two boys. One, (John Joe) would not know his father until he reached manhood. But another son, Michael, became his pride and joy. Born around 1933 to Minnie, Johnny had taken him into the mountains with him as soon as he could walk. A good-looking, intelligent lad, Michael would learn to love the outdoors just like his father, and Johnny could not have been happier.

By the time the surprise attack at Pearl Harbor plunged America into World War II, Johnny's guiding business had established connections with wealthy and reputable men who were often repeat customers year after year. In fact, the guiding business actually picked up during the war, as rationing forced men to seek elk for meat. Also, the demand for furs drove prices higher–a double bonus.

But up north in Alaska, the story was much different. Both Canada and America had suddenly realized the vulnerability of the Territory when Japanese assaults on Dutch Harbor and the occupation of Kiska threw Washington into a panic. After having ignored Alaskan defenses year after year and squabbling for fifteen over a road through Canada, it was evident the enemy now intended to seize this prize and expose the West Coast as a jugular vein.

Army posts sprang up quickly, and the floundering Palmer Project in the Matanuska Valley began shipping thousands of tons of foodstuffs to the military bases. Production could not keep up with demand, nor could the farmers keep help...farm hands quickly left their jobs for the high-paying construction projects, as did thousands of men in other careers. Almost overnight, a 1500-mile stretch of rough and treacherous road was carved out of Canadian and Alaskan forest and muskeg swamps, a mammoth undertaking laughingly called "the Burma Road of North America." Alaska was too busy with war to be thinking of moose racks and Boone and Crockett scores...

8
THE MAGNET MOVES

"Alaska did something to a man–its very name made one think of adventure, challenge, and wilderness..."

As busy as Johnny was, the annual few weeks of inactivity that always separated trapping from hunting could not be idle. Johnny had too many mouths to feed, so for a brief time, Johnny took a job in Utah working on the Geneva Project. Male workers were scarce during the war and pay was good. While he was there, news came that one of his Indian friends, Eugene Surrell, had been lost in the mountains:

> The Indians couldn't find him and they was good trackers, too. But because of their fear of the mountains, they only tracked him partway up and then quit. When they lost him, I was working down in Utah, and I said to myself, "I can find that guy." But I never went 'til the next year. I was going up around this lake and was trying to get into camp before dark and I stepped

over this log. The lake was real close, and there was a gun there under this log. So I grabbed it and went on into camp. Later, I was polishing it up with Oleo and getting it all greased up, and I looked on the stock and saw it had a real pretty carving with E. S. on it. I knew then it was Eugene Surrell's. I went back the next day. If I'd looked around the evening before I would have seen his bones and clothes. But I sure wasn't gonna break up my trapping to go report the find. He had a Mackinaw jacket, so I laid it down and put all the bones I could find and his clothes and a hat with fishhooks in it, and put it up in a tree and went on about my trapping. Then long about the first of April when trapping was breaking up, I went down to the Boss Farmer (a U.S. Marshall) and told him I found Eugene Surrell up there. So he told me to go up there and get what I could out. Well, overhearing all of this was this smart-aleck who was always in some kind of trouble with the law and was always bragging about how he could out-walk Johnny Luster anywhere, anytime. I just let him go on, but I thought to myself, "I'll take him with me," but I had it in mind to teach him a lesson he wouldn't never forget. Going up the mountain I got to thinking about it, how I was gonna beat him walking. I remembered that at a camp I knowed there was a bunch of Ex-lax. Well, I went over to the camp and got it and I come back and rubbed off the label–I didn't know this guy couldn't read or write. So I gave him one whole box of it and he ate the whole thing. I didn't go very far when I told him I didn't want mine; he could have it, too. So I gave him the other box. It like to have killed him! I didn't have one bit of trouble walking out first!

Johnny's love of pranks had still not diminished. The end of the war sparked a new age for everyone. Spirits were high, and there was a tremendous sense of urgency to get back into the pursuits that had been shelved in the duration. Now, one could get on with living.

News had filtered down into the Montana-Wyoming states about the Alaskan highway. It had been started at the beginning of the war as a supply route across the Northwest Territories to offset the vulnerable shipping lanes that were subject to Japanese attack along the Pacific and Gulf of Alaska waters. A deal had previously been made with Ottawa whereby the Canadian stretch would be turned over to Canada six months after the war was won. It would soon be open to civilian traffic.

Thoughts were churning in Johnny's head.

"I was always thinking, golly, I'd like to hunt some of those things they call caribou and mountain goats," he remarked to Luie Lanwhre, one of his friends he had hunted with many times.

A man of considerable wealth, Luie answered, "If you ever want to go up to Alaska, let me know; we'll go together!"

What a tempting thought...

Michael was now in Wentworth Academy–a prestigious school in the East. (A Catholic priest had arranged for this promising youngster to attend.) This bright, intelligent boy had taken to the woods with the same enthusiasm as his dad, and since the age of four had accompanied him while hunting and trapping, learning all he knew from him. But times were changing, and Johnny recognized it. The days of the big-game hunting guides were not going to be the same anymore. It was evident that government regulations over the wild animals would require a man to have a good education in order to pursue that vocation.

Freelancing guides like himself were going to be a thing of the past unless they followed the trend. Michael must first get his education, and then they could be together again. Johnny thought long and hard about it. Right now he had an established business. If he went to Alaska, he'd have to start from scratch. But Alaska did something to a man. Its very name made one think of adventure, challenge and wilderness–the same things that had moved four generations of Lusters Westward across America, and Johnny was feeling those stirrings with unexplained regularity now. Wyoming was not the isolated place it had once been. More and more old haunts and secluded canyons felt the steady footsteps of encroaching waves of people. The inevitable population explosion was already affecting areas once thought of as primitive back country. No place was now inaccessible.

Johnny astride one of his many horses in Wyoming–just before leaving for Alaska. The year was 1944.

As it happened, one of Johnny's friends was Will Simpson, prominent judge in Wyoming and also brother to the now-successful, but aging, Alaska guide Jimmy Simpson. Letters between the two indicated Jimmy's desire to get enough horses together to introduce the use of pack trains in Alaska. But since the animals were scarce and expensive, he had not yet found a way to do it. Will suggested Jimmy get in touch with Johnny, who was not only a first-rate guide, but also an expert horseman.

Letters were exchanged, and plans made for Johnny to come to Alaska, plus ship up some horses. Jimmy would send the money to buy the horses and arrange for shipment. The decision was made–they would go to Alaska:

> I was gone trapping way back in the mountains in Bull Lake Canyon. Nobody ever goes in there, but it's good trapping. I had Lillie and three of the kids with her, and I went down to get some groceries and it came...an awful snowstorm. I had a terrible time getting back to the top of the mountain that day. I had to use snowshoes. The border of the mountains was tough going–below there's no forest, and above it there's no forest. To get through that the snow's deep, and I brought a horse back 'cause I got word to come to Alaska, and I was gonna move Lillie and the kids out. Well, Lillie was a good scout, but she wouldn't always do exactly like I told her, and I had told her to stay there 'til I got back. When I got in there, she was tying things up and getting ready to leave, just because I was a few days late. She was safe as long as she stayed in the camp, because there was a big cliff sloping off, and back in there it was good and dry and there was some big spruce trees growed up right to the edge of it. It was a perfect place. I had always camped in there about a third of the winter, catching beaver. We had a place down in

Riverton, but we never stayed any place very long 'cause we was on the move; the mountains had me.

Johnny packed out Lillie and the kids and took what furs he had trapped to his buyer. "Now you're gonna meet somebody up there in Alaska that will put you under for sure," the man laughed.

"I know. They're really tough up there," Johnny answered.

He could only imagine how tough.

The first priority was the horses. Jim had sent him the money to purchase the animals and ship them up to Alaska, but it was a mammoth job which involved using airplanes to round up the wild, legendary Shoshone ponies. These small horses had been instrumental in the Lewis and Clark expedition a hundred years earlier. They were no beauties, but the best pack animals to be had. John, Jr. describes their peculiar disposition:

> Those Shoshone horses are real gentle and tough, but they're runny. I go out with those ponies, pack 'em and ride 'em, and other people can't touch 'em–they really take up to a person. If you're afraid of them, you'll never ride 'em. I got this one–if I'm out in the dark, I'll call him and he'll whinny to me.

Jim had specified (at the urging of his grandson) that he wanted nothing over 900 pounds, which proved to be a mistake. Fortunately, Johnny also selected five or six "good" horses and two of his own, including

"Smokey," his favorite. He had already contacted Luie Lanwhre.

"You said you wanted me to let you know when I was ready to come up to Alaska. Well, I'm ready," Johnny had written.

Luie immediately replied. He would pay for the trip up and furnish a milk truck for Johnny and his family to ride in.

"Be there shortly," he wrote.

Johnny had nicknamed Luie "Governor" due to the fact that Luie had once booked a hunt for the governor of Missouri and instead showed up himself. Thereafter, he had hunted with Johnny every year. A wealthy dairyman, he could well afford such luxuries.

Meanwhile, Johnny was busy arranging for shipment of the horses. Shipping horses to Alaska was nothing new. The discovery of gold in the Canadian Klondike in 1896 had put out a demand for pack horses, and the Colony settlement had called for the larger breeds. But it was still a risky business, and terribly hard on the animals. Many were lost at sea and tossed overboard before they ever reached the dock at Seward:

> There was 13 horses (wild ones) we shipped up, and the rest was mine. I put 'em on a railroad car in Riverton and shipped 'em to Seattle. Then they went on a steamboat to Seward, and then a train had them in boxcars and sent them up to Palmer at the depot. One or two of them died on the way up. A big old gentle mare, she died and they throwed her overboard. They said

she got seasick or something. Nowadays, they bring them up over the highway, or if they're rich, they fly 'em up.

Johnny related, "Governor soon drove up from Missouri with a gunny sack full of money, another man with him driving the milk truck and another rig with a brand-new aluminum boat towed behind." "I'm gonna fish them lakes all the way up," Governor explained.

Afraid she couldn't find them in Alaska, Lillie packed a couple of big washtubs and dutch ovens in the boat. She and the three girls would travel behind Johnny and Governor, who took the lead in the milk truck. They were now set to go; the caravan was ready.

There was quite a group sending them off: friends, well-wishers and family. Johnny's eyes wandered around him, carefully drinking in one last look at the place where he had been born and called home for over forty years. To the West, the Wind River Range was still snow-covered, the granite crag of Pingora Peak thrusting its white fingers into the blue sky.

June summer blooms were now coloring the meadows of sweet grasses, and the bull elk were now feasting. He would miss it all–the hidden and secret campsites only he knew, the solitude and beauty of Bull Lake and the friendly sheepherders.

But something had shifted. The Iron Magnet, that invisible force which had somehow caused men to leave their roots for other lands, had moved, and now lay way north in far higher mountains. Alaska seemed

Although barren and uninviting to most, the wide open spaces of Alaska and its plentiful game drew Johnny like a magnet.

to be a place where a man could get a fresh start–something Johnny, now in the prime of his life, desperately needed. It would be hard to leave those that had stood by him and understood his peculiar ways, but he was also painfully aware of his troubled life and the mistakes which had left him in constant turmoil, though he could never understand that his love of mischief and nonconformity was largely responsible for it.

But in spite of it all (whether out of envy or admiration), he had already become a living legend. For the rich and influential there was a certain amount of pride in knowing personally, a true mountainman, whose character was still lodged in the Old West. Yet there was a trail of tears he had personally blazed, in spite of his cries of persecution and intimidation. Both loved and hated, Johnny Luster was Johnny Luster, and no move to Alaska would ever erase it or change it one degree. But perhaps if he could find a higher mountain somewhere the new challenge would write a new and different chapter in his life...

9
THE CHEECHAKO

"There was something about this land that seemed to wrap itself around the heart of a man and intoxicate his senses..."

The "Alcan"—as the Alaskan/Canadian Highway came to be known—was a 1500-mile adventure in misery. Starting from the end of the Canadian-Pacific Railroad at Dawson Creek, B.C., it snaked its way over endless miles of swamp, frost heaves, glacial rivers and hard rock. As a military road, it had hardly been constructed with tourists in mind, and in 1948, it offered little in the way of highway hostels and emergency services. Consequently, after a brief opening, the number of highway breakdowns necessitated its closure until the following year. So, as it turned out, Johnny and his party would become some of the very first civilian travelers to make it through. Barely.

It would take them about two weeks before they arrived in Palmer around the fourth of July. The shiny new aluminum boat was lost–along with Lillie's washtubs and dutch ovens–when the trailer broke loose. But no one seemed to mind delays. Johnny remembers:

> It took us so long because Governor wanted to stop and fish every lake he saw. We stopped at Kluane Lake, the largest in the Yukon Territory, and they had to go fishing. I stayed behind and used up all the coffee getting acquainted with the local Indians.

This would only be the first of many trips up and down the Alcan for Johnny. Later, he would be back down into Canada for horses:

> I had asked Old Jim why he didn't get his horses in Canada, and he said, "Prohibitive!" Well, it wasn't, 'cause I went down later, when I got to be an Alaskan guide. I went down to Dawson Creek and bought horses a lot cheaper, already broke, for $25 or $30. I paid $60 for a bloomin' mule. That's what it cost me to get it across the line, because they had a high price on mules coming in, 'cause in the early days they had used 'em in the gold rush and they were real valuable. I run into trouble the time I brought up some horses on the Alcan. They was working on the road, but it was a lot better than the first time. It had been raining, raining. We had to go around some stuff, and the shoulder gave way on one of the trucks and the horses was all loose and it dumped 'em all out. Didn't hurt none of 'em, but we had to catch 'em. Then we had to sign a paper releasing them of responsibility

before they'd lift the truck up and get us through with a Cat. We was the last ones through then; they closed the road after that. We brought some 20 head and quite a few hundred little pigs. While we were held up at Watson Lake, I decided to go watch some fellows fish. I could see those fish swimming, and they was long-nosed. I seen one, and I went and got a board off this outfit and when I saw him come by, I hit him so hard, by golly, I got him! I had him hid under my truck seat and I went through customs and by the time I got home, that fish was stinking! But I got one anyway...

Jim had been pretty disgusted at the horses. They had arrived before Johnny did.

"He shoulda' knowed better," Johnny commented, "He let his grandson talk him into ponies."

But Jim was also upset because they were not broke, something he had neglected to tell Johnny he didn't want. This misunderstanding almost turned Johnny back.

"Well, there's your horses!" he stormed out, heading for the milk wagon. "I'll just go back to Wyoming!"

"No, no! Don't let me down!" Jim yelled quickly. He needed Johnny to break the horses and help with the upcoming hunt.

After some fence-mending and meeting-of-minds, the misunderstanding was resolved. But already, the other guides and local sourdoughs had their eyes on the little sawed-off runt from Wyoming. If horses

121

needed breaking, they would show him what Alaskans were made of!

One of the men spied the big gray. "I'll ride 'em; nothing to it!"

Everyone pressed in as the man mounted the animal. The horse reared into the air and with little effort, bucked the man off into a strawberry patch.

"Let me at 'em!" another cried, and struggled to mount the horse while others held the big gray. By this time a sizeable crowd had gathered to see the contest. As soon as the man was on him the animal roared into the air again. Johnny recalled:

> He had on one of those pretty sheepskin coats, and that horse rode him into a barbed-wire fence, throwed him off and tore up that coat. Old Jim went and rented some other horses from around the valley 'cause they was ready to get a hunt started. "You can just break 'em all in camp!" he growled at Johnny.

Lillie stayed behind with the girls in a tent pitched in the front yard of a guide's house while the men set out for Boulder Creek. It would be there that Johnny would have to prove himself to these Alaskan sourdoughs, and hunting was not the only thought amongst the guides and packers in Old Jim's outfit–Johnny Luster was. If he was such a hot-shot guide, mountainman, and wrangler, then he'd have to prove it by riding that big gray, and everyone was looking forward to seeing

Although Johnny was a "Cheechako" in Alaska, his knowledge of horses and the outdoors was as extensive as any "Sourdough."

him bite the dust. The great Wyoming-Alaska fight was on:

> Smokey was my own horse. I had never ridden him down in the states, but I had "pulled" his tail and put shoes on him 'cause I used him for a pack horse. I didn't have him ready to ride, because we had other horses we could use. Some of the men got to drinking the night we came into camp, and Old Jim told them, "Well, he'll ride that horse tomorrow morning; I'll see to that!"

Before retiring for the night, Jim stuck his head into Johnny's tent and issued the ultimatum, "You better ride that horse tomorrow; they're doing a lot of talk about you."

> I said, "Okay." So the next morning during breakfast, I stuck some pancakes into my pockets and went over and saddled up Smokey. They all saw me and gathered around to see the ride. I just picked up the bridle reins and walked off with the horse and left 'em standing there. I walked way down the trail into a kind of swampy meadow. I knew Smokey liked bread—pancakes or anything like that—so I would put him aside and start talking to him, feeding him those pancakes. Finally, I kept bribing him and working him out on the trail. I was down there so long that after awhile Old Jim came barreling down the trail on his horse, 'fraid I was hurt or something, and here I come riding up to him.

Well, we rode back together into camp, and boy, were they let down!

He was secretly breaking Old Jim and at the same time...

That summer of '48 was one adventure after another for Johnny. There wasn't any gold lying around to pick up like he'd thought, but Alaska was excitement! Wyoming was wide open country too, but the wilderness here was awesome:

> I couldn't see much when I first got here, but when we got out of the timber, I could see all of this game and I thought, "I'll just get us a homestead and stay up here. When Michael finishes up his school next spring, then we can really have a future in Alaska!"

There would be a mandatory five-year wait for him to become eligible to try for his Alaska guide license. He would have to supplement his income with trapping in the fall, but that was no problem for someone like Johnny. He had done it most of his life, only this time he would have to chart new territory. Jim didn't have enough guides to go around in September. Most of the men took off for the annual State Fair in Palmer and left him short-handed with several hunters still booked, including the writer for Outdoor Life, Charlie Elliott. They would need the horses the men took with them, so Old Jim sent Johnny to fetch them eight miles away...on foot:

I could run for miles and miles and not get tired, so I took off to the Fairgrounds, got the horses, and let them trot behind me coming back to Palmer.

No doubt that was quite a sight!

The next day was full of activity. The first priority was to get the men and animals into camp. Johnny, by now, had adjusted somewhat to being low man on the totem pole, although it was difficult for him to keep from saying his mind and be unable to lead the men in the hunt. But he would force himself to be patient and let things work out:

> I first met Charlie Elliott during that fall hunt. We were making camp when Charlie got up on this hill and looked and seen this grizzly bear and hollered for me to get the horses! So I asked Jim, "What about it?" And he said, "Get the horses, but you go along with them." He had been feeling kinda bad, so I went along with them.

What followed has already been described by Charlie Elliott in his "Tribute," a thrilling narrative best left to him to recount. The event was a hair-raising experience neither would ever forget. Johnny, in thinking back on it, knew all too well how close they all came to being bear meat. He reminisced:

> You never have time to think what you'd do. Like that little dog of mine; he once had himself a squirrel. That squirrel didn't have a chance

Johnny would lead many packstings like this one in his 40+ years as an Alaskan guide and trapper.

either, 'cause my dog was so close behind. A wounded bear–you sure don't play possum with 'em!

Jim was upset about the bear, because it was illegal for them to go out and hunt without a guide. Although Johnny was an experienced guide in Wyoming, he was not recognized as such in Alaska. Johnny remarked:

The old fellow was quite a cranky old bugger. He was still kinda funny until after the bear incident. We was cleaning up the camp and I thought I heard a wolf, at least I thought it might be a wolf. I asked Jim, "Does a wolf make a kind of 'bur-rrowin' sound?"

And he snapped, "If you hear a wolf, kill it!"– you know, cranky, grouchy.

I had an old Enfield one of the helpers had loaned me. It was like they used in the war when they was passing out guns. It had a big old battle sight on it, but it could really shoot. So I got out of camp and I saw this wolf walking up this bar, and I thought I would get a little closer. But the minute I stepped closer, he laid down. Then he stood up, and I knew he was gonna run, so I took a good bead and made a long shot and killed it deader then the dickens. I went over and tried to lift him up, but he was too heavy. So I came back into camp for a horse and Old Jim met me.

"Did you get the wolf?" he snarled.

"Sure, I just came back for a horse to pack it in."

Boy, everything changed then. He came in all excited and said to me, "Soon as we get things cleaned up here, why, we'll go over to Oshetna and go caribou hunting!" So everything changed then; we were friends from then on.

He found out I could do anything and some of it a lot better than the rest of 'em. After that, he couldn't do enough for me. After we got back into town, Old Jim traded a horse for a new Marlin 30-30 and gave it to me. Jim said it wasn't good for nothing, but I sure killed a lot of tough ones with that 30-30. He gave me a brand new .06 one time, and when I finally got my own guide license, I still had that old 30-30. The sight was bent, so I took a rock and straightened it up.

When I went to Anchorage years later, I had this Dutchman I hunted with a lot. I went down to Kennedy Hardware and he came out with this featherweight Winchester and said to me, "Here! We don't want you to get killed with that old rattletrap you got!" So I had a 30-06 for a lot of years.

The summer was over before they knew it. The riot of color from the fireweeds and meadow wildflowers had been spectacular, but had vanished almost overnight. Wild roses had shed their petals and produced the rose hips. Blueberries and wild raspberries were almost gone; the salmon had finished their annual spawn. Now it was time to think winter.

Johnny returned from hunting camp to Palmer and moved his family into a cabin on the Chickaloon River–part of an old mining camp. He would run a trap line that winter and come spring start his homestead there, thirty miles north. They were "Alaskans" now. Governor and his friend had fished themselves silly and had returned to the lower '48, as had the hunters. But they would be back, and Michael had written he would be coming the first of May. For the first time in his life, Johnny felt a peace and contentment; things were working out after all. Here was a chance to start over and perhaps someday get his own outfit among people who seemed to think like he did. There was something about this land which seemed to wrap itself around the heart of a man and intoxicate his senses. Johnny Luster had been smitten with Alaska...

The Luster children grew up with their father's love of the outdoors and everything it had to offer. The income from these pelts helped support the family during the winter, between the hunting/guiding seasons.

10
NEW BEGINNINGS

"A virgin bride awaiting her bridegroom..."

It was a struggle for Johnny to describe the incredible beauty of the land that was now home. "Breathtaking" and "awesome" were words totally inadequate. Palmer, though a more picturesque setting could hardly be found, was but the doorway into a country so dazzling and majestic it almost didn't belong on earth at all. Barely five miles from the city the ground suddenly gave way to an open chasm so deep and frightening, one was caught off guard. It came as a complete surprise to know you had been on top of a mountainside all the while.

The glacial Matanuska River of silt snaked its way down the valley floor, its turbid gray rapids eating their way towards the sea. To the north, roads led into gold and coal mines near the village of Sutton. But it was this river whose origins—some sixty miles upriver in the 27-mile long glacier—separated two tremendous mountain ranges–the Talkeetnas on the north, and the

Chugach on the south. It would be here, along this cut into the earth, Johnny Luster would find his home. There could be no better place for this last mountainman. Streams and rivers worked themselves down the slopes and lay like fingers on a giant's hand: the King's River, the Chickaloon and the Moose River...Granite and Caribou Creek. Strange-looking peaks appeared suddenly out of nowhere: Pinnacle, Castle, and King's Mountain, dwarfed by the monstrous ranges on either side. It was an enormous area, filled with bear, moose, caribou and the lovely white Dall sheep; a virgin bride awaiting her bridegroom.

The mountains of Alaska were teeming with game like this Rocky Moutain goat. Outside hunters would pay top dollar for the chance to hunt these animals with a competent guide.

Although Alaskan seasons were short by most standards, spring bear hunting was allowed and provided additional time each year Johnny could make a living as a guide.

Johnny now put himself into the trapping season. He had not brought any of his traps up from Wyoming, and without traps there would be no trapping:

> I had to buy about 30 traps, then when I was out one day I came across a bunch of traps that had been abandoned, so I took them and started a trap line. I went to the head of Boulder Creek (about 25 miles) out across and went down to the Matanuska River, then ran a short line up the Chickaloon.

Johnny's wife and some of his children in front of their home. Pelts from his trapline adorned their house until they could be taken to fur buyers in town.

He would have to do it all on snowshoes, for as yet he hadn't acquired a dog team and sled–these were Alaskan ways of doing things:

> I trapped lynx, wolves and quite a few mink. Mink was real high then, plus I got around 100 weasels worth $2.50 each.

Alaska was new Territory with a lot to learn. Yet Johnny adjusted well. Since childhood he had that sense of adventure that always made him wonder what was on the other side of the mountain, and there were certainly plenty of mountains around here! But other guides didn't quite understand that, and still considered Johnny a "Cheechako," an Alaskan term for "greenhorn":

> I went up with one of the trail hands looking for the horses one time, but it soon became apparent to me that he wasn't doing much looking for horses. Instead, he was looking for something to shoot. He wanted to show me how much he knew and how much I didn't, so he went and got a couple of sheep way up on the mountain and when he came back down he said to me, "I'll let you have one."

'Course he did that so he wouldn't have to pack it down. He gave me the big old ram and he kept the dry ewe. The whole thing was illegal. He thought I would have an awful time with that ram since I was so small, but I was a lot stronger than I looked. I cut the thing all up and put it in a big old army pack and we headed back to camp. When we came to the Chickaloon River, there was a big old tree pole across the stream, and he told me, "Here's how you cross the river on a pole," and he tried walking across it. He got about in the middle and started wobbling and fell in. Now it was my turn. I sat astraddle of that pole and pushed myself across and got to the other side with my pack of meat without a drop of water on me.

He chuckled:

When he got over the river dump, he never gave

me any more lessons about walking logs. But it was all I could do to keep from laughing.

That winter Johnny met some hunters who were soldiers stationed at the military bases in Anchorage. Johnny began taking them into the back country for ptarmigan and other small game. He would have to wait several more years to take them on big game hunts, but for now this would supplement his income.

The men loved the scraggly mountainman who not only was a trail-wise hunter, but a delightful humorist as well–a man you learned something from. He explained:

> When you shoot birds, you can save some shells
> if you'll get lined up and get the head of one
> and then wait, and when one goes past the other,
> you can get two with one shot.

He seemed to delight in teaching the Indian ways of doing things, combined with what he would learn in later excursions into the Talkeetna and Wrangell Mountains. Johnny was fast earning his reputation and forming a base of clientele who would become regular customers when he finally got his guide's license.

Michael was excited at his father's letters from Alaska—it sounded like heaven on earth—and if things worked out like they planned, he would be coming up the first of May. It was a promise of great days ahead. The Alaska Territory was really only waking up, and to get in on the "ground floor" was all a man could ask for. He was almost through with school, maybe he

Johnny's hunting skills plus his humor—like roping a porcupine— made him a favorite with the hunters he guided.

could get on with the Game Commission or something. At any rate, he and Dad would be together again, doing what they both loved with a passion.

Michael folded the letter and stuffed it back into the envelope, he would answer it later. Right now he had to hurry; he and a friend were going to go flying with this man, and he was excited. Returning war pilots enjoyed taking civilians out to show off skills they had learned in combat battles, but the small planes around Riverton were not made for dive-bombing exhibitions, especially by men who had already had too much to drink.

The tiny aircraft roared as it accelerated towards the ground, and the pilot started his pull-up too late. The tip of the wing caught a fence post and careened directly into a house. A huge ball of fire instantly engulfed them, killing everyone. There was no escape. As soon as they could, someone ran and put a blanket over Michael's face and took his hand, but it was too late.

It was April first, exactly one month before he would have left for Alaska.

The news of Michael's death was a devastating blow to Johnny, something he never quite got over. It was especially painful to be unable to attend his funeral; they didn't have the money for a plane ticket. He would have to work out his grief the Indian way, but that second summer would be terribly hard.

Old Jim already had things lined up for spring bear hunts. Johnny had been amazed at his way of doing things:

> He didn't guide like the rest of 'em; he was always dressed up in suit clothes. And he didn't

go for nothing but real rich folks. He'd get a lot of letters and sort 'em out. He could tell. If it was real good writing, them's the ones he'd contact. Doctor's can't write—I don't know why that is—and some of 'em that isn't educated, they got the best handwriting.

Johnny's children didn't always have the finest clothes, expensive toys or possessions, but they were happy. He worked hard so they had the necessities of a good life.

Johnny's wives were, of necessity, hard-working, and creative just as he was. This pet black bear substitutes for a puppy.

There was also the homestead to clear and a house to build, so Johnny had plenty to keep him busy and his mind off Michael. Lillie was pregnant again and due anytime. So much to think about! He decided to take her with them into Boulder Creek. Dr. Ashfall would be in the hunting party with them, just in case.

She had not been all that happy so far, though the prospects of a home of their own brightened her spirits. But Lillie suffered from deep emotional problems as well, from a childhood of abuse. There were times when she had wandered off and left the children to fend

Johnny always watched out for his children. They learned about horses and the outdoors at an early age.

for themselves, something Johnny was always apprehensive about, so he took no chances now. She needed him, yet he had to work, and this was all he knew. Until the kids were old enough, he would have to be close by.

So Stella was born in hunting camp on Boulder Creek. She would be followed by Hilda the next year, then finally another son (John, Jr.) and two more daughters–Lisa and Norma. The Chickaloon homestead was a beautiful piece of property. Some twenty acres had already been cleared–good meadows for the horses. They built the house from old lumber at the abandoned gold mine. There was no electricity, but the place was warm and comfortable. His son John, Jr. remembers those days:

> Livings were pretty easy. We grew our own potatoes and shot our moose, and that was a living. We never had no electricity and I never saw a movie until I was like sixteen, so it was a different kind of life. When we did start going to school, we wore Max tennis shoes and people laughed at you and talked about how poor you were. But it never bothered me because I remember thinking we were rich because we had 160 acres and 80 horses. And you'd hear them talking about how their parents were having a hard time feeding a horse, and we'd just throw hay out to 'em. Even though my shoes weren't like theirs, I had a lot more wealth than they did.

144

Husky puppies like this one were destined to be working dogs, pulling Johhny's sled along his winter trapline. Here, John, Jr. plays with a puppy before it joins the ranks of sled dogs.

Two years after they came up to Alaska, Old Jim suffered a heart attack and died. That would be the end of that business, and Johnny would be forced to wait it out for another three years before he could take his exam. Some of the handlers chided him, "You'll never pass the thing; the most you could ever be is an assistant!" He surprised them all and passed it on the first try.

Johnny had not wasted the time in-between. He still took the Elmendorf and Ft. Richardson soldiers

Johnny's reputation as a top-notch guide brought him a surplus of hunters without the need to advertise. This hunter took a nice caribou on an early season hunt.

hunting and had acquired some good horses from them after they had used them for pack trips. Governor was still coming up every year, and he had never failed to make an impression on Old Jim's clients:

> I've been loaded every year since I got my guide license, sometimes too many. My first non-resident hunters were two couples from Florida. Someone told 'em about me.

There would be little need to advertise his services. Some of his first ventures were far into the Chugach and Wrangell Mountains:

> I used to go up there bear hunting. I'd take some

John, Jr. grew up in a similar manner to his father–also learning to love and understand the outdoor life. This pose with a grizzly bear is evidence of his hunting skill at an early age.

people with my sled dogs (acquired after several seasons), which we'd use as pack dogs. We'd boat across the river and put packs on the dogs and go; it was a lot of fun. To me, the whole world's been funny–if I couldn't cook up something to be funny, why, to heck with it.

He laughed, his blue eyes sparkling:

The area was teeming with bears. Them grizzlies; you don't try to shake hands with 'em–they're liable to slap you. I never trust 'em. I never got hurt by 'em, but I hurt a few of them. I had one come up to my sleeping bag, and I thought it was a horse. That was up the Chickaloon, and I had three hunters and they was all in

Cabins needed strong doors to keep out marauding bears. These paw marks indicated how large the bear must have been to reach to the top of the door.

this tent, curled up, lined up sleeping bag, sleeping bag, sleeping bag. So when the bear come up, I thought, "That wasn't no horse!" We had a moose hanging up quartered by the camp and that bear took one of those quarters hanging up—with those guys sleeping there—and was eating on it. He took off when I got up, and I went in the tent and said, "There's a grizzly out

Even the stongest of doors can't keep out all the bears. Once inside, they will get into every single item in the cabin, biting into every food container as well as most non-food containers, just to make sure no goodies are left behind. Cleaning up the mess can take days.

here!" and they didn't get up, just kept on sleeping. So I kicked each one of 'em in the hind end and shouted, "There's a grizzly out here!" So they jumped up and seen what was happening. Of course they didn't go back to bed after that!

Another time, we had cooked up a big mulligan stew so we'd have things ready when we came back from 30-Mile camp. We had to go up and get some horses and when we got back, a bear

Johnny's hunters were successful on many bears and probably took most of the nuisance bears who robbed game meat or destroyed cabins.

had raided the camp and eaten up the mulligan, all the food and even some of the canned goods. So I laid for him that night. I put my gun beside me, and sure enough he come up to the

*Johnny's trouble with bears usually ended in the bear's demise.
Although his reputation may have been embellished at times, he
wasn't afraid to tackle a bear with only a knife, or an axe, if that
was all he had at hand.*

foot of my bed. Dumb me, I shoulda waited until
he got right up and shoved it up against him
and pulled the trigger, but I was a little bit leery,
so when he was about six feet away, I shot. But
it was dark. I shoulda shoved it right against
him; it woulda given him an awful surprise that
way. Well, I cut some blood out of him, but it
had to be a flesh wound. We had to wait until
daylight to track him, and he went across this
steep hill, leaving a good stream of blood. But

it was just a flesh wound, 'cause if it'd got inside, he'd never went up that hill. He never came back to rob the camp.

As soon as young John, Jr. was old enough, Johnny began taking him along, the same as he had done with Michael years earlier. "I learned everything I knowed from him," John admitted. Now a guide himself, John, Jr. reflected on some of those experiences:

There's always every year you're out in them woods with the animals. There's always those times when the hair on the back of your neck feels like barbed wire. Dad taught me early not to waste bullets; when a bear charges you, you save your bullets. You don't shoot to make noise. I had one with a .300 one time. The bear spinned and leaped, and I bolted the rifle again and it come at me and I fired, and I left and came back when my knees quit running! I woulda stayed there, but my legs wouldn't let me. I hit it only once out of those two shots. Dad had the mumps one time, down on the coast. I was about ten years old then, and I had a .308 Winchester. Dad went up into the brush to chase out a bear for a hunter to shoot it, but it didn't chase and he got to hollering it got him, and I ran up there and killed that one. I shot him about six times and he rolled down and was charging again when I shot it right in front of me. Dad said I killed it the first shot.

John, Jr. with one of his (pet) dogs Mike, by one of their classic trapper cabins. The snowshoes and antlers were integral parts of their life, not just brought in for decoration.

Johnny, because of incidents where there was no alternative, became famous for using axes to kill bears.

153

Johnny spent much of his time on the Chickaloon River–wild country where moose and bears were plentiful. Horses made access easier, but required skilled wranglers and constant attention.

One such foray had taken place in his corral back in Wyoming, but there was a hair-raising escapade that took place with his two sons:

> I got two boys, both named John by accident. One of 'em I hadn't seen since he was two weeks old until 24 years later. They brought him into Chickaloon–his mother had kept track of me. Boy, I had a crazy life! Anyway, we all was out going over the pass. I seen the bush pilot, Loren Wiederkehr, and I told him we were going over the mountain and we'd see him on the Chickaloon. And he said, "Yea, we'll see you over there tomorrow." He didn't think I'd make it.

> Well, we had been to look the trail over and bring some wood back up to the top of the mountain camp. We forded the river and got wet.

> I said to the boys, "I'm hungry; let's go down to camp." So we did, and really stocked up on food.

> Well, we cooked up something to eat and was sitting there eating and getting dried out a little bit when John Joe says, "Look! There's a grizzly!"

John, Jr. describes what he saw:

We was cooking up some beans on the fire and my half-brother John Joe hollered, "There's a bear!" and even though he was older than me, he was new up here. Every time we'd seen any bear they was up in the blueberry meadow. So I knowed that, and I immediately looked to the blueberry meadow across the river, and the bear wasn't there. It was coming right into the camp where we was at!

In between all the bear encounters and guiding hunters, Johnny still had time to do a little hunting himself. John Lackey (l.) and Johnny(r.) with three 40-inch Dall rams.

Johnny shouted, "He's right here!"

The huge animal ran right at the three men, less than 100 feet away!

"We're had boys, grab an axe!" Johnny shouted.

All the guns had been left in camp on top of the mountain, some three miles away.

John, Jr. was sitting on a log between his father and John Joe. "They like to have knocked each other down passing one another, and there was an axe sitting right beside where they were at," Johnny recalled.

The elder Luster grabbed a fire axe and ran toward the beast. John Joe grabbed two axes, one in each hand, standing there totally frozen in fear.

"This isn't any way to fight a grizzly at all!" John, Jr. thought to himself while he ran for the nearest tree:

> I knew that was the thing to do. I decided every time you're in camp with hunters they all fight over who gets the bear. I decided I'd be the sportsman and they could have it!

Meanwhile, Johnny reacted quickly. He remembers:

> I thought I'd try to make it to this partially built cabin and jump up on the roof so I'd have a chance at him. I ran barefoot over there, and while running I happened to remember what an old Frenchman told me. He said if you rattle a bunch of cans it'll scare a grizzly to death. Well, the roof we had on that cabin was tin, so I hit it with the flat of the axe just as the bear was right

As a guide, Johnny also had to know all the hunting regulations and follow them carefully–something he sometimes found difficult. But Johnny was also a good source of information for game wardens because of his extensive knowledge of the outdoors and because he spent so much time on the trail. Here, Johnny is providing useful information that will help this warden solve one of his cases.

there ready to come up over the bank. All of a sudden, that bear was gone! I played "Yankee Doodle" on that roof 'til he went out of sight!

"We got em' boys!" Johnny hollered.

He looked, and there stood John Joe, totally frozen, with both hands in the air holding two axes, not a sound coming out of his mouth.

"Dad said he was saying something, but his mouth was froze. That bear coulda come up to him and took those axes and eat him up right there," John, Jr. recalled. Johnny laughed:

I looked for John, Jr. and I heard a little squeak coming from somewhere, and I looked up and saw him in the very top of a tree. If he'd of climbed any higher, he'd been climbing air!

"Of all the warriors I've had, I'da thought you'd been right beside me," Johnny scolded his younger son.

"I woulda been, if you'd of come up the tree with me," John, Jr. answered.

"He tells it that he passed two squirrels going up that tree!" Johnny snickered.

Johnny continued:

Speaking of bears, we had this bear—one of the biggest—tear up a camp up on the creek. I was kinda straightening up the camp and a backpacker passed me as I was coming down over Slop Hill there. On the way down I came upon these two do-gooders (the kind that don't want nobody killing nothing), and they was telling me how I shouldn't be shooting animals. Well, I looked, and I seen that backpacker starting up the hill and not more than 40 yards behind him was this bear, going like the devil, his hair straight up on him! He was going to kill that backpacker! Well, I jumped off my horse and I had a little .44 rifle and two shells and those do-gooders started yelling at me, "Oh, you're not gonna shoot him are you?"

Well, when the bear heard them, he started coming for us. I met him on the creek and when he got right across the water, I hit him. It turned him, and he got going down the middle of the creek. He was so big, that even though the creek was kind of high, he was clearing the water! I got the other shot into him in the ribs, but I tried to get him in the heart. Well, he went on down the creek. So I got some of the boys there at Chickaloon the next day and we took them people out (I had two hunters from Ohio), and then we went back up there. We figured he must have got washed away.

Well, in just a little ways, that bear jumped out and charged them. The youngest hunter knocked the tops out of the trees, but the other one knocked the bear down, and when he got up, he finished him off. And he was big!

Johnny's skill with horses allowed him to travel through some of Alaska's most rugged country and succeed as one of only a handful of horse-string guides in Alaska.

11
THE CHICKALOON MOUNTAIN MAN

"When all was gone, there would be nothing left but a scar..."

Alaskans, by their very nature, are survivalists. There is no inch of ground anywhere that is not threatened at some time or another by earthquake, flood, fire or other natural disaster. It is a harsh environment, whose extremes of heat and cold test the limits of one's endurance and fortitude.

But it is these very things which serve to separate the men from the boys and determine the select group which are its permanent citizens. Once it discovers one of its own, it is not because of what he or she says, as much as what he or she does that earns respect and admiration.

Johnny, though a transplanted guide who could not claim to have lived with Alaska's special challenges all his life, nevertheless conquered them one by one, and in so doing became eligible to join a select group of men and women deserving the reputation of true Alaskans. Tourists who paid thousands of dollars to see Alaska expected "The Last Frontier" to contain some grizzlied, bearded sourdoughs with the ability to tell a good tale and keep a tenderfoot from looking silly—and much more, to fulfill the wealthy hunters with dreams of stuffed moose heads over their fireplaces.

Hunters coming to Alaska had to depend on their guides' skill to keep them alive, as well as to have a successful hunt. Johnny could not only satisfy both of those requirements, he excelled at them.

Johnny fit the mold perfectly. For he had learned long ago that nature was seldom tolerant of ignorance, and could be totally unforgiving of stupidity. It was because he had already survived these lessons in the wilds of Wyoming that he could survive what Alaska had to offer. Though it was, and is, a land raw and unconquered, that very fact would be the thing that gave such a man a reason to live, and created the drive that motivated his existence.

Johnny Luster had no idea why, but throughout the ensuing years in the Alaskan wilderness, he managed to become a fond subject of various writers. As early as 1954, magazines such as the Alaska Sportsman, Outdoor Life and Sports Afield got wind of the legendary mountainman and featured him as a larger-than-life folk hero–which he was. Men who hunted with him hurried back to their city desks eager to share their adventures and photographs with the rest of the world– as many of his clients came from abroad. Johnny fit their image of the mountainman perfectly, and his exploits and sense of humor made him all the more interesting. The older he got, the more valuable his stories.

Alaska had been a good thing for Johnny, and the people of Palmer had accepted him and his family, something the tight-knit society of pioneers did not always do. Perhaps the publicity helped.

Just after he had gotten his guide license, he was featured in the Alaska Sportsman in a six-page article by Foy Stevenson entitled, "Johnny Luster of Chickaloon," which mainly emphasized his trapping ability. He had not yet come into his own as a recognized big-game hunter. But three years earlier he had already set the record for Dall sheep, bagging one at Boulder Creek with a horn over 54 inches!

John Butler wrote about Johnny's hunts in the same magazine, both in 1958 and in 1963. Other articles began appearing in the Anchorage Times, the Daily News, the Greatlander, and the Alaska Hunting Journal.

But notoriety was not what Johnny was looking for, or even interested in, though it was seldom far from him. Challenged by an Austrian to come up with a moose rack bigger than the one in Vienna's museum, he took the man out and found one with a 75-inch spread! Such feats did not go unnoticed.

His children, though torn apart by Johnny's tumultuous marital affairs, seemed to gyrate towards their father and to his way of life. Psychologists might have a hard time explaining how his children managed to somehow become successful and well-adjusted individuals. John, Jr., a real estate broker and guide himself, tells of his childhood:

> Dad was nearly always up in the mountains. I got pictures when I was about two years old riding in a box on the side of a horse. Time had no meaning to us. I knew we were considered poor, but we really weren't. At the time, I didn't realize other people had money, and went to the store and bought bubble gum and stuff. We

166

Two of Johnny's children—Stella and John, Jr.—with one of their father's first guide trucks. Their childhood was not the normal one for their era, but they thrived under their father's guidance.

never went to the store, and when we did finally go, it ruined us. I never had any money in my pockets—never wanted any—maybe matches you could use. Then I can remember the first movie I ever went to; it was Swiss Family Robinson at that theatre in Palmer. It scared me to death 'cause it had that bunch of logs rolling down, and I was sitting right on the front row and it scared me to death! Bob Mumford, he had the barbershop in Palmer at that time, and Dad had been gone for over a year, so Mom moved into Palmer and got a little rental house and put us on electricity. Now we was "city" people, and I got a job cleaning up that barbershop because I wanted to go to that movie house. I went in and asked him if it was okay if I swept his barbershop and straightened things up so I could get the money to go to the movies. I can remember him looking at me kinda funny, "You're too old for this," but he gave me 50 cents. It cost 35 cents to go to the movies, and I'd have 15 cents for popcorn. Boy, I was excited! Then after that, I told him about the movie, and he realized I was serious about it, so I got a steady job there for awhile. I went to see that same movie three times!

His marital affairs still taunted Johnny, however, until he and Lillie finally split up. He ended up remarrying Jan, only to separate again. It seemed that wherever he was, Wyoming or Alaska, there was always an assortment of wives and children left lying around as the end result of his inability to forge together the mountainman with the 20th century. Yet other guides had made their living in much the same way without such problems, and one could point to that fact as proof men could do it. But Johnny was not the ordinary guide; he was also Indian–"All Indian inside," as he put it. Nor did these other men choose to live in the same place they worked, but usually maintained fine homes in the cities.

No one could ever doubt where his love really was; he was married to the mountains. They held him spellbound, with a web so tightly wound they were the very sinews of his soul, and he roamed over them as a vaga-

Johnny's first love was the mountains–here he travels through his Chickaloon River country that he called home for fifty years.

Horses made crossing Alaska's numerous glacial rivers much easier.

bond relic from another time. Even his family, like most of his clients, only shared brief visits with him and then returned to their modern lifestyles and comforts, leaving him once again with his obsession. It was a lonely life, yet this same uniqueness opened doors others could only dream of. There were other reasons for his love of the solitude of those mountains. They were his refuge from trouble, from confrontation with a world that did not operate with many of his self-styled principals and sense of justice.

The old days had scarred him, perhaps permanently, in such a way that he knew within himself that he did not belong. Johnny confirmed that fact on sev-

Horses also made packing game meat—like these caribou quarters—much easier.

eral occasions. Once, he killed a drunk man who was brandishing a gun and threatening to kill his own children. To Johnny, he was only doing what had to be done at the time, with no more impunity than when he killed attacking bears. For any other person to have done it, there would probably have been little said, but Johnny Luster had a past, steeped in the violence of range war days. Though finally ruled as justifiable homicide, such incidents gave him all the more reason to keep to himself as much as possible.

He was uneasy around people he didn't know. Once, when he attended a church service, he asked af-

Johnny always belonged in the wide open spaces, far away from the confines of a schoolhouse or a big city. Alaska had exactly what he needed.

terwards, "How did I do?"–his deep, blue eyes searching for childlike approval.

Yet, ironically, this same man found himself the object of adoration and honor, and wherever he went, Johnny would find himself recognized as someone different–someone the younger generations admired and respected. When seated in an economy-class seat on a flight one time, he was sighted and instantly moved to first-class accommodations. The stewardess had been one of his clients!

Honor was not easy for him to take, and he felt uneasy in the fine homes of wealthy clients who begged

Johnny hollding a small bear trap.

him for visits. Yet at the same time, his sense of adventure kept him traveling to see, to experience all that life was about–strangely curious about how other people lived, perhaps as much as they were about him. It would be such curiosity that often opened unexpected doors others could only dream about.

It took a lot of persuasion to get him to explain a picture of President Reagan among his letters. When he and his daughter Hilda decided to tour the Eastern states, they happened to visit the White House. While looking around, someone spotted the bearded mountain man, and he ended up being introduced to the then-President Reagan: "He invited me to come down to the ranch in California sometime to ride horses with him," Johnny modestly admitted.

Johnny's interests were not limited to hunting and trapping. He also had a keen interest in rocks and minerals, and led manned, pack trips into the mountains, simply to look for thunder eggs or fossils. One of his biggest finds was picked up by the Associated Press when he and his two sons found a rare fossil near the Chickaloon homestead. Was there anything in the mountains he did not know about?

The success of Johnny Luster lay not in his business sense, nor in his contacts with influential people. It was his abilities that made him what he was. His friend Charley Elliott spoke about it in an article he wrote for the Atlanta Journal in March, 1986 that answered a question, "Who is the best woodsman in America?" Johnny, by that time, was in his eighties:

...this question really intrigues me. To begin with, what qualities make the kind of outdoorsman who might compare favorably with our pioneers and mountainmen of several generations ago? Today there may be some who can get along without the modern conveniences and have enough pioneer traits to maintain themselves in any isolated situation, but they are by no means abundant.

At least one man, Charles Elliott, thought Johnny was the best woodsman in America. Certainly many of Johnny's clients would agree with Mr. Elliott.

What qualities, for instance, are there to satisfy such a title as "best woodsman"? Here are those that occur to me, though not necessarily in this order.

Whatever his age, a man should be vigorously tough. In traveling from place to place, an early frontiersman ran all day, or as long as necessary. His physical condition was superb. He endured extremes of weather with callous contempt. His exceptional traits of woodsmanship included the eyes of a bobcat, the ears of a fox, and both the experience and ability to quickly interpret what he heard or saw. Every leaf or grass blade out of place told him a story. Unusual noise got his attention. He could track any creature that moved. With his rifle, knife, and knowledge of the outdoors, he could live comfortably off the woods under any circumstances.

The only man I know who fits that description is John Luster, who lives in the mountains above Palmer, Alaska. John is in his 80's and the toughest hombre of any age I ever met. I first hunted with him when he and I had an uncomfortably close fracas with a grizzly in 1948. I was with him a couple of years ago, and hopefully will be there again this year.

At his age, he can climb all day in the mountains and then all night if necessary. He's a guide and outfitter and lives in the Talkeetna Moun-

Johnny was active into his eighties and beyond–the classic, tough outdoorsman forever.

tains a large percentage of the year. He guides fishermen and sightseers in the summer months and hunters in the fall. With his dog team and sled, he runs a 100-mile trap line in December and January when the temperature often dips to 50 and 60 below zero. He lives in his shack that he calls "Fort Starvation" at the head of the Talkeetna River.

Most of the year on his outfitting trips he doesn't live in a cabin or tent, but spreads his sleeping bag under a fir tree with close, sloping limbs and branches that shed water like a rooftop, so that the ground around the trunk is always dry.

When he's hunting, he sees everything that moves, and I'm sure everything that does not move. No track escapes him. He is exactly as I imagined most of the old mountainmen of earlier days must have been...

As Johnny reached old age, he mellowed into a philosophical, wise man, not quite sure that his way of life was such a bad thing. He realized that many of the youngsters (including some of his own grandchildren) were growing up in the cities never knowing anything about responsibility or hard work. He was very proud to have "turned several around" by taking them with him on trips into the wilderness. Johnny proudly exclaimed:

One of them, he was rebellious and all. Well, I took him out with me, and when he got back home, the first thing he wanted to do was help

One of Johnny's many, happy caribou hunters.

with the dishes. He started making good grades
and is now studying hard–hoping to be a guide
someday, too.

Several of his children, including daughters, are
considered to be great hunters and guides themselves,
and annually make trips into the back country with their
father. Johnny recalled:

The kids growed up, and Fay and Bonnie got
married. My sons-in-law, they flew over to
McCarthy one day and they come back telling
me, "Boy, that is the country!" So I throwed a

hunt over there. I had a lot of hunters that year, so I split the outfit and sent some of them over to McCarthy with guides, and then I run guides out of Tonsina Lodge over on the Copper River. Well, I did all right, but they didn't do so good over at McCarthy. I flew in nine horses by plane and paid for it...

Nothing made Johnny any happier than to see his brood growing up to appreciate the incredible beauty of Alaska and learning to revere what it represented to him, even if they did have a lot to learn!

Johnny was always exploring different areas of Alaska with his horses, but it was hard, risky work that didn't always pay off.

During the winter of 1984, Johnny took his grandson, Eddie, and two of his friends up the Chickaloon to

Johnny enjoyed taking clients and his family out to appreciate the Alaskan outdoors and camp life he loved.

take pictures of mountain sheep. What followed came to be one of the most remarkable stories ever told:

> Eddie was in the Navy, but home on leave, and so we decided to go up the Chickaloon. I wanted to go look for a place to set wolverine traps up this 14-mile canyon, which was sheer ice at that

time of the year, but we went up anyhow. Eddie saw a bunch of sheep, so he and the boy from New Jersey climbed up, wanting to get some pictures. I went on up the creek and looked it over where some people had a mining camp at one time, and on the way back we looked up to see Eddie and them was stuck up on the rim and didn't know how to get back down.

So I climbed up to help them find the way, and we was letting ourselves down over some different waterfalls with a long rope that we had brought with us. We would double it and put it around something and slide down, then take the other end of it and pull it down. At the last waterfall, the worst one, the other boy had already run on ahead, and I was trying to hurry those two boys down because it was the 21st of December, and those days were short and cold. Well, instead of going around it like we should have, they went down right over it, then jumped and turned. When it came my time, I put my hand on two flat rocks standing vertically, just high enough for my head, but when I stepped down in there and started to jump, my feet slipped and flew out and I went over sideways. Then I flew through the air down another ten feet and lit on my back, right where I was gonna jump. It must have pulled the leg right up and out.

Johnny hollered at the boys, "I broke my leg!" They thought he was joking and kept going, but he called them back, "You better get back here!"

Jay had already gone far ahead, but he was the strongest of the three and could help the most.

"Get Jay and get him back here!" Johnny told the two boys.

They could see that Johnny was lying on his back right under the waterfall with his legs crossed, the broken one lying across the other. It was obviously broken.

Winter activities in Alaska are particularly risky, but Johnny continued trapping and guiding throughout the year–as any true woodsman would.

After Jay returned, the three boys tried lifting Johnny. The minute he stood up, he got sick, and there was no way he could drag the leg–they would have to go for help

"Head right out and get that rescue outfit to fly in here, Jay!" Johnny told him. "I can't move."

Darkness soon fell on the two boys and Johnny. Eddie took part of a sleeping bag and wrapped it, as best he could, around his grandfather. It wasn't long before the water began to run over the place, but it was impossible to get him off the ledge:

> If I'da been human, I woulda died, 'cause I was getting cold. I was cold from the start, but that water running around me probably kept me from freezing to death. But I was thinking to myself, "I wonder how long it's gonna take for me to get to that place where you don't think about nothing no more–you just go to sleep and die?" But I never could go to sleep. I just lay there and shook.

Eddie began to sob. Johnny tried to let him know that his granddad wasn't giving up. In the darkness, Johnny knew he mustn't let the boys lose heart, and began making up a song:

> There's an old man back in the mountains. Now he's busted up his leg and they think he's gonna die, and look at poor Eddie, he's now gonna cry... That boy from New Jersey, he went nuts, he went crazy! He was crying; "Eddie! Eddie!"

Johnny and his son, John, Jr., bundled up against the cold of the Alaskan winter.

But Eddie came and sat beside of me. He was upset, but tough enough to take it. My back bothered me where it was broke. I can't lay straight anymore, because my head is pushed out in front of my body.

The hours went by in agonizing slowness. Johnny's thoughts slipped back in time: to all the grizzlies, a lifetime of gunfights, beatings, drownings and being thrown from horses. Was death going to come from an accident after all of that?

A cold, dark reality, so frightening it cannot be described, suddenly came over the old mountainman.

Eddie had broken the gunstock off the gun when he jumped, but it could still shoot. Johnny reached down and picked it up, handled it, then set it down:

> I was wondering, you know, how some dumb buggers like that would take that gun and shoot themselves. No, I'd never do nothing like that; I don't care what death I die. Different ones I've known that had cancer, why, they shot themselves, but my belief was, God didn't intend for you to take your own life–no way at all. I figured I was gonna die. I couldn't figure out any other way how they was ever gonna get back in time before I'd freeze to death. I couldn't build no fire nor nothing. The boys, they just didn't understand packing wood and stuff like that. I coulda did it. I coulda took a rope, and made a bundle and put it on my shoulder and went up there and got the fire going, but you couldn't tell 'em nothing they could understand. But they sat up there and was suffering too...

It was late afternoon the next day when the rescue helicopter arrived at the canyon:

> I thought, "There's no way they can take me up over that canyon the way that we come down." Everything got quiet, and they made two passes, then flew off. Well, I thought, they just couldn't do it. I thought, maybe I'll freeze to death yet.

Johnny's tenacity for life allowed him to live a long, adventurous life and survive to see his children grow up. In his nineties, he poses with his son, John Eston (Jr.).

With only five hours of daylight today, there's not much time left.

Pretty soon somebody hollered, "You alive up there?"

"Yes! I'm alive up here!" Johnny hollered back.

The rescue outfit had climbed up the canyon with a stretcher:

> They climbed up there and put me on a stretcher and strapped me down, but as they started down, they were slipping and having trouble packing me out. I said, "Why don't one of you go up and get that rope that's lying there and fix it on each corner and then have it long enough that on a level spot you can pull this thing." So that's what they did, and there was this one slide with a big rock in it right in the middle of the canyon. They had to lift me up, and I remember I was standing straight up and somebody on the other side caught the rope. They finally got me in the helicopter and took me to the hospital. I was there about two weeks, and walking in a few days with crutches.

Miraculously, Johnny had survived 19 hours in sub-freezing temperatures, lying with a broken hip–at age 80!

What was it inside of this man that seemed to hold tenaciously to life, when others would have simply accepted their fate and died? It was a lifetime of personal encounters over and over again with the possibilities of death, and yet having seen that there are inner re-

One of the many things Johnny learned from the animals he hunted was to rest when you have the opportunity. Here he is taking advantage of a warm summer day to catch up on his sleep.

sources in each of us that we only discover we have in such times of testing.

Johnny had seen it happen over and over again in his long years of challenging the Dark Specter. Most often it would come at the sacrifice of his own safety to save the weak and fearful caught in situations they could not handle–like the time he crossed an ice dam in Caribou Creek with his sled dogs and turned around to see the man following him with his team suddenly panic halfway across. Wading up to his chest in the freezing waters, Johnny managed to save the man and his team, only to develop pneumonia and almost die of an allergic reaction to medication.

"My clothes was so frozen they had to be cut off me," he said. "A lot of men would have turned 'toes up' about that time..."

But by now, time was running out, both for Johnny and big game. Statehood had brought significant changes for the Alaskan guides. Gone was the five-year, mandatory wait and the apprenticeship requirements that had assured qualified and experienced men, and subsequent regulations had only served to destroy a once highly-respected profession. The days of the mountain woodsman, with his keen instincts and age-honed knowledge were fast disappearing as balloon-tired airplanes and roaring snow machines invaded their once-protected guide areas. Sadly, he reflected on the times:

Johnny as guide and woodsman.

There's not much game left now. The real hard winters kill off about 50% of the moose population, and they now have a cow moose season which only kills the goose that lays the golden egg. Wolves have all but killed off the sheep, and the do-gooders don't want to kill the wolves. 'Course they've never got to watch a wolf eat a caribou alive...

Would there ever be another mountainman? Had the time come for the passing of an era—to relegate it to legend and tale on the shelves of libraries—a part of history that once lived, could never again find purpose or use in an age of high-technology and computer satellites? Were men seeing it all vanish, as herds dwindled, not because of excessive numbers of guided hunters, but because of the mismanagement and ignorance of "specialists"? Would it all end because of mismanagement by "experts" whose textbooks were often written by men who had never hunted nor spent a day among the animals–like men who deal in oil futures, having never seen a drop of raw crude?

Quite possibly, Johnny Luster was casting a shadow into the valleys below him, reminding the younger generation that the sun was behind him and tomorrow, when it came up again, he would be gone. Just as the mighty glaciers were retreating from their ice-age domination, leaving behind them barren and eroded shale, when all was gone there would be nothing left but a scar where this mammoth giant once had his pathway. Those with any foresight could recognize it.

The lack of wolf control was one of the most significant causes of the drastic decline in Alaska's wild game herds. Johnny did his part, but one man was not enough to control the voracious wolves.

EPILOGUE

"A wandering star on a jouney through time..."

The old mountain man is out today. It's July now, time to get the pack horses ready for that trip up to Caribou Creek.

I noticed he'd been doing a lot of work around the place: built some flower beds and terraced part of the hill. Looks real nice. John, Jr. had strung a fence along the bottom of the pasture and cleared off a nice area for the dogs. Johnny's kids really seemed to care for him a lot.

Nobody was home, but I remembered the last time I came over for an interview. He was over the hill at John, Jr.'s place helping clear off some of the pasture of brush.

The mosquitoes were so bad! I saw he was busy and started to go, but he motioned to me. "Don't go, these darn mosquitoes are eating me up. I can't use none of those repellent stuff. Let's go over to the cabin." He was glad to get away, and I almost felt like he wanted to say some things.

Packing the bags for one more trip.

So we sat down at the little table one more time, and Johnny began to talk about the coming trip:

Hope Charlie Elliott can make it up from Georgia. He's had trouble with his eyes–getting old, too. They operated on him, but he still can't see good. I told him somebody would bait his hook for him. Boy, that guy loves to fish! There's a hundred lakes back in there with fish this big! I tried to give him one of my eyes, but he wouldn't accept it. We're gonna have a big time up there, grandkids coming and all. It's really something back in there!

I don't know why they call Caribou a "creek" and call King's River a "river," 'cause Caribou Creek is just as big as King's River and it's really wild if it takes a notion to be wild. The King's River never gets so wild that you can't cross it. I've hunted and been all over the Talkeetna Mountains—part of the Chugach and the Wrangells—I know them pretty well. I used to go up there bear hunting...take some people with my sled dogs and use them dogs as pack animals and go. It was a lot of fun!

To me, the whole world's been funny. If I couldn't cook up something to be funny, why to heck with it.

"What are you planning for the fall, Johnny?" I asked.

Guiding looks to be pretty good this year. I always got a stack of letters. Right now John, Jr.'s wanting me to hold up 'cause he's got some kind of big deal, but I'm not gonna take a chance. I'm gonna make sure I'm booked up this year. This may be my last year

Age was taking its toll on the old warrior. "Are you gonna trap this winter, too?"

Yeah, I plan to pitch a tent up the Nenana River. I'll build a really good one, and it'll be nice and warm. Might have a couple of guys come up and stay with me.

Johnny with hunters and their trophies. Memories like these are what keep mountainmen going.

The Nenana, I thought. It gets 40-50 degrees below zero there in the winter, sometimes colder. And he's 86?

Sometimes one doesn't have to say anything with words; there are unspoken signals that are given off. Johnny had just lost one of his old buddies. They were dying off.

Shuffling around a pile of letters, he pulled out a slip of paper.

"Would you like to read something I wrote when I was down with my friend Lester? I was with him when he died..."

"Sure," I answered.

"It ain't spaced right, I know," he apologized.

I picked up the paper and read Johnny's thoughts:

Here's to my old hunting pardner, Lester Besson: I set with him 'till he went to the happy hunting ground. God seen he was getting tired and a cure was not to be, so he put His arms around him and said "Come with me." With tearful eyes we watched him slowly fade and slip away. Although we dearly loved him we would not make him stay. A golden heart stopped beating and hard-working hands to rest. God broke our hearts to prove to us that He takes only the very best. John A. Luster.

It was a magnificent tribute to a close friend.

Johnny had often talked about death and dying many times during our visits. They were simple, folksy, but also messages he wanted to convey to his family and friends–his way of saying "goodbye" just in case he ever went back into the mountains and never returned:

> My mother always taught us kids to pray. We'd all get around the bed when we was kids and kneel down there. I prayed every night. If you happen to be in bed and something hits you, then you gotta get up and pray again.

> I know for sure there is a God. They'd have to kill me to make me say different. I'm not afraid to die. It might be kinda painful to be put to death for saying it, but they'd have to go ahead and do it.

> I hope when it' s time for me to go that John, Jr.'s there. I'm gonna go, "Boo-oo!," 'cause I'm not afraid to die. There's no use to be afraid. I figure if I belong to the Lord, why He'll do something with me. I just hope they let me in up there, 'cause if they won't let me in, I know the devil won't have me either, 'cause he'll figure I'll raise too much trouble down there. So I'll just wear out everything between here and there.

He chuckled:

> Heaven's one place you can't sneak in, they kinda keep that place guarded pretty well!

Johnny with two of his most trustworthy companions.

I've seen death so many times...come so close to it, myself and other people. People that commit suicide, they've just completely wiped it out. I got a funny feeling—from the Indian inside— that I would never want them to cremate me. It looks to me like it's not so bad if you've got a grave somewheres and some of your relations come there and put a flower on it. Whether or not you know it, it's a good feeling.

I want to be buried on top of Castle Mountain. That would be good for the kids, too, when they're trail riding and stuff, with me there on top. Maybe there'd be a family graveyard on top of Castle Mountain. They'd say, "The Old Man's buried over there..."

Someone had started the story that Johnny Luster could outrun a horse (which wasn't true, of course). But this and other stories spoke a great deal about this intriguing man. The "impossible" had always been his challenge–the spark that ignited his motives and actions, just as men climbed the highest mountains simply because "they were there." Johnny could not easily turn away from such conquests, and though such ideals were high principals taught to be admired in all the schools of philosophy, no one had foreseen it so engrained in a man's spirit that it might destroy his ability to live and be accepted as a "civilized" being.

It was not that there weren't other guides and scouts with many of his same abilities, but Johnny possessed another ingredient which was his and his alone: he was like one of the animals themselves, a lone wolf with instincts and age-honed intelligence that had allowed him to survive when others did not. They could have learned from him.

Hunting with Johnny Luster was not just a safari–it was an educational experience. He often shared his secrets with those wise enough to listen:

> You need to hunt like the Indians do, not like white men. White men take three steps and listen once. The Indians take one step and listen twice.

Johnny.

A descendent of the Shoshone ponies Johnny brought to Alaska to fulfill his dream in "The Last Frontier."

Johnny giving instructions on how to pack a horse.

Or he might caution the novice not to shoot a bear when he was above him:

> Bears will come charging downhill and end up on top of you, and don't bother with one that's been feeding on fish; you can't eat his meat.

Who could question the wisdom of an old man who had survived avalanches, blizzards and encounters with bears? This was a man who had fallen into frozen rivers with his dog teams, broken nearly every bone in his body, survived without food for days, yet kept returning time and again, ever wiser for the experience. An old man who, on crutches, still led a client over a mountain to take a trophy sheep.

He could cure a horse when the veterinarian called it a hopeless case, or fashion a fishhook out of the same horse's tail and catch his supper. To Johnny, it was only his way of life; to others, these were awe-inspiring revelations.

Could it be that he was destined to be the last mountainmnan, driven by the power of the iron magnet as it moved, like a Providential act, across America and stood as "finished" in the ultimate beauty of Alaska? Hard men to understand, they had served to stretch a scraggly hide from the Atlantic to the Pacific and from the Bering Sea to the Gulf of Mexico, not because of cities they may have built or any battles they may have won, but because their eyes were upon the mountains. They stood as conquerors to the weak and fainthearted in the valleys below: a silent statement of determination and faith.

In his bloodstream lay the particles of many peoples who had fought one another in bitter conflicts, yet also struggled together to build a powerful nation from the ruins of their hatred and violence. He had seen and been a part of it all.

His lifetime had witnessed the death of one culture, and the birth of another. Yet in his sunset years, it is ironic that the world has suddenly focused upon its inability to live in harmony with his environment, shocked to learn how little it knows and understands about nature's rules and laws. Perhaps he was wiser than all of us will ever know...

He would never fit the mold of the ordinary. It was almost as if he never really belonged to his generation at all, but had been left as a wandering star on a journey through time. Perhaps he was a reminder to those of us fortunate enough to have known him, of that special ingredient in the men who made this land what it is today, and that if we ever lose it, we will have lost our very heart and soul.

In reality, he was a man born two centuries *Out of Season...*

Johnny Luster
Alaska's last great Mountainman

BIBLIOGRAPHY

Kentucky, by Stephen A. Channing, W.W. Norton & Co., N.Y.

Wyoming, A History, by T. A. Larson, W.W. Norton & Co., N.Y.

Exploring the West, by Herman J. Viola, Smithsonian Books

The Trailblazers, by Bill Gilbert, Time-Life Books

The Great West, American Heritage, N.Y.

The Struggle for Tennessee, by James Street, Time-Life Books, N.Y.

Indian Cavalcade, by Clark Wissler, Sheridan House, N.Y.

Society and Thought in Early America, by Harvey Wish, Longmans, Green & Co., N.Y.

The Road to Shiloh, Time-Life Books

Beaver Dick, by Edith Thompson, Jelm Mountain Press

This Fabulous Century, Time-Life Books

*The Sweep West*ward, Time-Life Books

The Way to the Western Sea, by David Lawrence, Harper & Row, N.Y.

Sioux Indian Religion, by Raymond DeMallie, University of Oklahoma Press

POETRY BY
JOHN E. LUSTER

The following poems were taken from *Alaskana*, a book of poems by John E. Luster.

John was born in Palmer, Alaska in October of 1951. He was an only son raised with seven sisters. He was the third child from the youngest. His father, Johnny Luster, was a big game guide and trapper. His mother was a Cherokee Indian from Oklahoma. He was raised in Chickaloon, Alaska without running water or electricity, where he also became a big game guide (Master Guide License #77).

John fell in love and married a schoolteacher from Texas. It was with her help, that he learned to put his feelings on paper.

Alaska

It's north to Alaska, in search of pure gold.
It's north to Alaska, where the rivers run cold.
Where the summers are green and filled full of life.
Where the winters are brutal, without a good wife.
Wild roses and bluebells, fields red as fire.
Our state's scenic beauty makes a heart never tire.
There's caribou, moose and white mountain sheep.
America's tallest mountain and the night of the longest
sleep.
One runs a trap line, the other drills for oil.
A life filled with promise and laden with toil.
Our mornings are parkas, mukluks and cold weather gear.
Our evenings are logs in the fireplace and Christmas-like
cheer.
Once used to the cool life, one can't take the heat.
You live in a country without a named street.
One never dreams of freedom, when you've never been
penned.
When you look at the horizon and you can't see the end.
If you've not seen Alaska, or felt her yen.
Then now is the time, let your journey begin.

Alaskan Nights

With the North Star shining, so bright overhead.
The Northern Lights dancing, blue, white, and red.
The moon seemed to smile when it came out in full.
The love of the north land seemed to tug and to pull.
A spine chilling moment when the timber wolves howl.
Or just before dawn breaks, the hoot of the owl.
The sight of the polar bear out on the floe.
Or the spray of a whale, when he comes up to blow.
To ride on a dog sled in the midnight sun.
From Anchorage to Nome on the last serum run.
The silence of the runners as they glide through the snow.
The breath of your lead dog as the moon makes it glow.
Red of the sunset as it fades from the skies.
Oh the gift God gave us–the use of our eyes.

Maybe Next Fall

Well here's hoping you're working hard and staying
stressed,
That way hunting season seems the best.
If the phone's always ringing, and the mailbox is full,
Then dream of the campfire and shooting the bull.
With no meat in the freezer, or new horns on the wall,
I'm keeping my chin up and thinking next fall.
Our children still love us, our women still care.
While I'm thinking rabbits, cause I'm fraid of them bear.
Sheep on the mountain, moose on the hill,
Winter's set in and brought on a chill.
My wife is still pretty, and teaching at schools,
She's keeping me busy, and buying me tools.
My dog's hair is curly, my horse lost his gait,
Maybe next fall I'll use him for bait.
The bear are too many, and the moose are too few.
To even the balance depends upon you.

My Sisters and Me

Only once we were young, and we were truly free.
Only once we were young, my sisters and me.
We would chase the rainbows to find that pot of gold.
It must have been just out of reach, from the stories we
were told.
At dawn, we dreamed of ponies, and oh, how we could
ride.
With our pockets always empty, we filled our hearts with
pride.
We never had electric, natural gas, or oil.
What we had was firewood to make our water boil.
With no food on the table, and no food on the shelves.
We learned to hunt and forage, so we could feed our-
selves.
We never shared a glass of wine, or knew of summer ice.
But the time we shared with loved ones, now that was
worth the price.
Yes, once we were young, and we were truly free.
Yes, once we were young, my sisters and me.
We might walk for 20 miles, or snowshoe through the
night.
But, we all grew up knowing what was wrong and what
was right.
Our yard was filled with clover, wild berries on the hill.

When mother spoke of berry pie, a pail we'd quickly fill.
Sometimes it was fireweed, or homemade clover honey.
It was one of the things my sister learned, cause we never
had no money.
Have you ever mushed a dog team, or coasted on a sled?
Have you ever had a sleeping bag? We had one on every
bed.
Have you ever whirled twenty feet of wire around above
your head?
And when you threw the wire up, two mallard ducks fell
dead?
Jesus must have helped me out. I know that tale is true.
With so many mouths to feed, he knew we needed two.
Yes, once we were young, and we were truly free.
Yes, once we were young, my sisters and me.
Have you thought of all the things you lost, when you lost
your childhood?
Now that you're buying gasoline, instead of burning wood?
What about that deed of trust, or the taxes that you pay?
We used to stay at spruce trees, a new one every day.
Now you're just expected to have shoes on your feet.
Back when we were young, horse manure softened up our
street.
Yes, once we were young, my sisters and me.
I finally found that pot of gold.
It's called my memory.

TONYRUSS.COM

Guiding you to Success in the Alaskan Outdoors

ORDER FORM

All books are fully refundable; satisfaction is guaranteed.

Sheep Hunting in Alaska - 2nd Edition, by
  Tony Russ, Softcover-$22.95, Hardback-$29.95
Bear Hunting in Alaska, by Tony Russ,
  Softcover-$22.95, Hardback-$30.00
The Manual for Successful Hunters, by Tony Russ,
  Softcover-$24.95, Hardback-$32.95
The Quest for Dall Sheep, by Jack Wilson,
  Softcover-$19.95
The Johnny Luster Story, by Mary E. Adams,
  Softcover-$19.95
Moose Hunting in Alaska, by Rich Hackenberg,
  Softcover-$22.95
Alaska Bowhunting Records, by Tony Russ,
  Hardback-$15.00
Alaska Wear, By Tony Russ,
  Softcover-$15.95

BOOK TOTAL...................................... $_____
SHIPPING by air ($4 for 1st book, $2
each additional book; International - $_____
approx. double these fees) ....
TOTAL ENCLOSED .... $_____

Name:_____

Address:_____

City:_____State:_____Zip:_____

Telephone:_____

email address:_____

Send check or money order to Northern Publishing, P.O. Box
871803, Wasilla, AK 99687. Or visit **www.TonyRuss.com** to
order with a credit card, plus see our other products and
services. Contact us at tony@TonyRuss.com.

TONYRUSS.COM

Guiding you to Success in the Alaskan Outdoors

ORDER FORM

All books are fully refundable; satisfaction is guaranteed.

Sheep Hunting in Alaska - 2nd Edition, by
  Tony Russ, Softcover-$22.95, Hardback-$29.95
Bear Hunting in Alaska, by Tony Russ,
  Softcover-$22.95, Hardback-$30.00
The Manual for Successful Hunters, by Tony Russ,
  Softcover-$24.95, Hardback-$32.95
The Quest for Dall Sheep, by Jack Wilson,
  Softcover-$19.95
The Johnny Luster Story, by Mary E. Adams,
  Softcover-$19.95
Moose Hunting in Alaska, by Rich Hackenberg,
  Softcover-$22.95
Alaska Bowhunting Records, by Tony Russ,
  Hardback-$15.00
Alaska Wear, By Tony Russ,
  Softcover-$15.95

BOOK TOTAL..................................... $_____
SHIPPING by air ($4 for 1st book, $2
each additional book; International - $_____
approx. double these fees) ....
TOTAL ENCLOSED .... $_____

Name:_____

Address:_____

City:_____State:_____Zip:_____

Telephone:_____

email address:_____

Send check or money order to Northern Publishing, P.O. Box
871803, Wasilla, AK 99687. Or visit **www.TonyRuss.com** to
order with a credit card, plus see our other products and
services. Contact us at tony@TonyRuss.com.

TONYRUSS.COM

Guiding you to Success in the Alaskan Outdoors

NORTHERN PUBLISHING

ORDER FORM

All books are fully refundable; satisfaction is guaranteed.

Sheep Hunting in Alaska - 2nd Edition, by
  Tony Russ, Softcover-$22.95, Hardback-$29.95
Bear Hunting in Alaska, by Tony Russ,
  Softcover-$22.95, Hardback-$30.00
The Manual for Successful Hunters, by Tony Russ,
  Softcover-$24.95, Hardback-$32.95
The Quest for Dall Sheep, by Jack Wilson,
  Softcover-$19.95
The Johnny Luster Story, by Mary E. Adams,
  Softcover-$19.95
Moose Hunting in Alaska, by Rich Hackenberg,
  Softcover-$22.95
Alaska Bowhunting Records, by Tony Russ,
  Hardback-$15.00
Alaska Wear, By Tony Russ,
  Softcover-$15.95

BOOK TOTAL..................................... $_____
SHIPPING by air ($4 for 1st book, $2
each additional book; International - $_____
approx. double these fees) ....
TOTAL ENCLOSED .... $_____

Name:_____

Address:_____

City:_____State:_____Zip:_____

Telephone:_____

email address:_____

Send check or money order to Northern Publishing, P.O. Box
871803, Wasilla, AK 99687. Or visit **www.TonyRuss.com** to
order with a credit card, plus see our other products and
services. Contact us at tony@TonyRuss.com.